I am Alice

I am Alice

Break up. Breakdown. Breakthrough.

Alice Readman

I AM ALICE

Break up. Breakdown. Breakthrough.

Alice Readman

Published by Travel with Alice Publications

This is a work of non-fiction. However, to preserve anonymity, some of the names of the people portrayed in this book have been changed. My aim is not to upset any of my friends or family members in the writing of this book, but to portray a set of circumstances that I experienced during a short period of my life between 2014 and 2015. I hope by sharing my experiences it will give hope, understanding and compassion to people who read this story.

ISBN: 978-1-7391558-0-3 Paperback
ISBN: 978-1-7391558-1-0 Hardback
ISBN: 978-1-7391558-2-7 ebook

Library of Congress Control Number: 2023903843

First Edition Published 2023

Illustration & Cover Design: Sarah Bonnar

For my parents for instilling resilience
and love in my heart that
never wavers

Contents

"What you seek is seeking you"
—Rumi

Preface

On a crisp, sunny day in April 2009, I walked down the aisle in a simple long white dress with my big brother Tom, feeling anxious. After my dad passed away when I was 32, I had always wondered if this day would ever come and who would take his place on my wedding day. I was grateful to have found Andy through a close friend and it had worked out perfectly so far. I imagined an exciting new beginning, but it felt a little odd that I was getting married in a Catholic church. I had cameras flashing in my eyes from my friends and family, who enthusiastically took pictures of us, as we walked down the aisle in an old 1930s-style church, just like the one my Catholic parents had married in.

The moment I stopped in front of the altar, with the priest staring down at me, something unexpected happened. Time seemed to be passing into slow motion. Momentarily my body felt floppy and I could barely stand up. I was wearing high heels but I could feel myself slipping. It was as if I was about to faint or a weight was drawing me down towards the floor. Staring down at the rustic red tiles, I felt a stabbing pain in my heart and was having difficulty breathing. My brother had a tight hold of me and Andy, my soon-to-be husband, grasped me on my other side. I was there but somehow stuck. "I've never seen you like this," Tom whispered, tugging on my arm. I couldn't answer, I was still frozen.

My eyes began to water, and I went to grab my handkerchief which floated down towards the floor too. I couldn't grab it, I couldn't move. I watched it fall, as one of my bridesmaid's rushed over to pick it up for me. It was the handkerchief my mother had given me for the wedding day, a special one, which had been my dad's.

When I came back to reality, I heard the priest saying to the congregation, "Alice is losing it." Momentarily confused, I felt shaken to my soul, as if someone had walked through my body, but I had made it back. I had already gained some unnecessary attention with my odd behaviour or maybe no one even noticed?

We sat down on our seats at the back of the altar listening to the service and having to face everyone in the congregation. Slightly shaking, I waited for my heart to slow and clutched Andy's arm. I was confused about what this meant. I just kept on telling myself to breathe and relax. Sitting under the brightest rays of white light, as the sun poured through the beautiful stained-glass windows, I somehow composed myself.

Five years later, on 30th September 2014, in a blink of an eye our marriage was over, and he was gone. It was like a dream, as though it had never happened at all.

1

A Moment in Time

One September morning in 2014, as the sun peeked through the blinds in our bedroom it promised a gorgeous day to come. Everything was in place for the new life that lay ahead for my husband Andy and me. We had child-proofed the house, bought toys, and decorated our two spare bedrooms so they looked like places children would feel at home. At first, I was a bit wary about the enormous responsibility we were about to take on, adopting two children under three, but equally more excited than I'd ever been about anything.

Their names were Isabella and Alfie. I'd fallen in love with them before I even saw a photograph of them, the moment I heard their names. They were names I would've chosen myself for the cutest pair. It still seemed unbelievable that I was going to be their mother. After five years of marriage and nearly as many years of trying to get pregnant, my lifelong dream of motherhood was about to begin. In just 24 hours, we would be in the same room with them for the first time.

As I lay asleep in my bed that morning, everything was ready to go. We would be meeting our adoptive children, three-year-old Isabella and her 18-month-old brother Alfie the next morning. I was planning to spend the day attending to final errands and finishing touches. I'd been told that Isabella loved painting and trampolining, so I had paints ready to be unpacked and I was set to pick up a mini trampoline from a local eBay seller.

Instead, at 6:30 am, I was roused from a sound sleep by Andy, who was standing over me, dressed in a grey-checked suit. Most days, he'd just give me a quick peck on the cheek before leaving for work, often when I was still asleep. But this morning, it was clear that he had woken me up purposely to tell me something. He knelt beside me as I rubbed the sleep from my eyes. He had done the same thing when he proposed, waking me up from a nap after I'd been unwell to ask me to be his wife.

Sitting up in bed, I smiled up at him drowsily, as the realisation of what day it was flooded back to me. Just one day to go. But my husband didn't smile back at me.

"I have feelings for Helen," he said matter-of-factly. His words made no sense to me. I knew who Helen was—another teacher at his school. In fact, I had been attending her book club for the last six months or so. The meaning of his sentence was incomprehensible. There was no way I had heard him correctly.

"I have feelings for Helen," he repeated, "And I don't want the children."

I just sat there blinking up at him. Surely, if this was actually true, we'd have had a conversation about it like two normal—awake—adults.

"Helen and I have been texting, and her husband found out."

"Can I see the texts?" I heard myself ask, from my half-asleep daze. I think my reasoning must have been: if this were true—which still seemed impossible—then I needed some concrete proof, something to jolt my mind into wakefulness.

"No, I deleted them."

"When did you have the time to have an affair?" It was the first thing that came to mind. Andy often stayed behind after school to finish off his planning and marking papers. As assistant head teacher, he had a large workload and always told me he couldn't possibly get home before 7 pm. If I ever asked if he could come home early, he got quite moody about it.

“Oh, I found time here and there,” he said lightly.

Things had been tense between Andy and me for a while. A few months earlier, he had gone on a two-week trip to Uganda, for a collaborative project between his school and a local one there. Helen had gone as well. Meanwhile, I’d been busy sorting everything out for the upcoming adoption.

When he’d returned, I’d noticed the change in him. He seemed sullen and standoffish and hadn’t told me much about the trip, but I’d read all about it in the blog post he had written for the school. There was a description of a day spent “building mud huts with the children and then watching the stars at 3 am with Helen.” He’d written that it “had been one of the best days of my life.” I knew then that something wasn’t right. Helen was a middle-aged married woman with three children, whom he referred to as his best friend at work.

That morning, as I sat in bed dazed, trying to process what my husband had told me, that he was having an affair and didn’t want the children we spent two torturous years trying to adopt. I thought he must be having some kind of breakdown. Stunned into silence, I looked around the bedroom where we’d slept for the last four years, at the newly selected furniture and fittings, the calming teal colour scheme. It had taken us so long to decorate since we could never agree on anything. Every little detail had to be carefully negotiated for us to both be happy with the result. The room looked real. But I couldn’t wake from this nightmare.

All I could think of was the children they were expecting us the very next day. I loved them dearly. In my heart, I felt they were already mine.

Had he just said he didn’t want them?

“What about the children?” I asked after a while.

“Sorry, I don’t have time to discuss this. I need to rush to school and see the head before Helen’s husband Frank gets there first. Frank’s going to tell the head that I can’t teach their son Josh.”

Andy had been teaching at the Round Hill Primary School

since 2009 and he had worked his way back up to the leadership team after coming in on a freelance contract. He'd had to leave his last job quite suddenly, due to his inability to meet the standards of the head, who had put him on a disciplinary report—he'd been given the choice to leave or be removed. It was a stressful time since we were in the middle of renovating our house and I'd just had my first miscarriage. So it was wonderful that he'd gotten back into the leadership role at his new school. Everyone there seemed to love him. He taught year six, the top class of the school. He also taught sport and ran after-school clubs showing films. Whilst at the school he had taught Helen's older children, Emily and Benedict.

It shocked me in those first few moments to think that his only concern was for Helen's son. But later I realised it was all about Andy saving his own skin, and his position in the school. He was just hankering to get downstairs and out the front door.

"What actually happened between you and Helen?" I asked, still not believing that he fancied her. I'd felt no threat from her at all. She and I were so different. She was very mumsy and traditional, while I thought of myself as a more free-spirited, creative type. I had trusted my husband, and I'd trusted her.

Secretly there was something I'd always found quite unattractive about Helen—she always seemed distant and superficial, even a little boring. I had never bonded with her at her book club, where I felt like a disinterested observer. She had an unnerving babyish voice—maybe working with kids you end up sounding like them. But I'd told myself not to judge her too quickly. On the surface, she was a sweet-natured, hardworking teacher, who had been married to Frank for 18 years and who loved her three children. I thought of her as a nice, ordinary, everyday sort of person. Her husband was in sales, and they'd had some ups and downs in their relationship, but nothing that would indicate she would just go off with my husband—never mind at such a crucial time in our lives. I knew she usually went sailing with her kids at the weekends. Andy had taught all her kids and often spoke about them.

"Helen stayed over last Saturday night," he admitted coyly, "but she slept on the sofa downstairs." As if that made it okay. "I cooked her dinner," he said.

This woke me up a little more. Andy had cooked Helen dinner at our house while I was away. They sat and ate in our dining room, surrounded by the new toys for our adopted children. They'd spent the night under our roof. I was shocked that they both felt that it was acceptable to do this.

He wouldn't tell me what the text messages he'd been sending to Helen said—only that her husband had been reading them. But instead of hanging his head or asking my forgiveness, he said angrily, "Her husband hacked into her phone and read her text messages. And that's illegal."

As I sat there listening to my husband, dazed and distracted, I reached for my phone and sent a frantic text to my sister Sara: My husband has just told me he won't be having the children. He's admitted to having an affair with Helen and loves her, and now doesn't want the kids! Please come over today. No Children. No Husband. Help! xx

Meanwhile, Andy grabbed his phone and wallet off the bedside table and walked out.

I jumped out of bed and followed him downstairs and begged, "Can you please stay home from work today and discuss our marriage?"

Just before leaving the house, Andy turned and looked at me, "You would've made a good mother."

Standing by the front door in my stripy pale-pink dressing gown, I was trying to wake myself up enough to understand what had just happened. Everything was flashing by so fast.

Glancing out the window, I looked up at the sky and felt like it was going to come crashing down on me.

2

I Lost Myself

Sara had texted back saying she needed to take her son Joe to school and would hop on a train down to me. I was relieved. More than anyone, Sara knew how excited I'd been about the children and understood how devastated I would be by this possible loss. An hour later, just after Andy went out the door in a flash, she texted she was waiting for the train. Knowing I would be spinning out, she sent another text, Clear your head of running future stories and focus on moment to moment. Remember you're a beautiful person.

Alone in the house, I didn't know what to do with myself, wandering around from room to room, trying to stay calm. So many thoughts clamoured for attention in my head. How could he do this to me? And without even having a proper conversation about it? How long had this been going on? How could he treat me like this? How could he suddenly not want me or the family we had been working towards for the last two years? I needed answers desperately. I had been ejected from my life, rejected by my husband, and cast away like an old shirt.

I couldn't deny that Andy had changed once he'd returned from Uganda. Even my sister had noticed it, pointing out a moment when she made a little dig at me and he didn't stick up for me.

I had written the following to him in my journal, with no intention of ever showing it to him: Since returning from Africa, life hasn't been the same. I feel you're not yet back with me and are still over there. I'm happy that you're passionate about something, and you can share that with someone like Helen. You talk to me as if I was your mother, rolling your eyes at the slightest thing, not showing the love and affection you used to. I feel you find me annoying, and you'd prefer me just to be quiet and not bother you. I talk too much. I was walking on eggshells all holiday and still am. We do things together, but we are separate. I don't feel a connection; it feels like you don't want to let me in. You are an island, and I am the sea washing around you, not making it to the shore. What have I done to you?

In the meantime, as I wandered around the house aimlessly like a ghost, Sara texted again, Alice, just try and relax! How was I supposed to relax? I put some bread in the toaster, then forgot to take it out or eat it. I made a cup of coffee and left it sitting on the counter. I decided to have a bath. My frenzied mind flashing with thoughts, I forced myself to focus on the moment, on the warmth of the water and the perfumed scent of the bubble bath. As my body sank deeper, I felt myself merge into nothingness. Did my husband really say those words to me, or have I lost my mind? Maybe the stress of the adoption has got to him, and he's lost it. Or maybe I've lost it. Or maybe I've imagined the whole thing, and my husband went off to work as usual?

I had to find proof. I had to speak to Andy. He couldn't just go to work and pretend nothing had happened. My heart raced faster and faster.

Lying in the bath, I thought back to our last holiday in Greece, only a few weeks earlier. I sensed something was amiss—all the signs were there but somehow, I chose not to see what was in front of me. We travelled to the beautiful island of Kefalonia for a week together for a break before getting the children. I saw and felt a different husband. Andy had spoken a lot about Helen.

On the first night into our holiday, we went out for dinner in a little roadside taverna and, over coffee, he said, "Helen's such a great teacher and such a great mother, and so undervalued at school."

"Oh, a bit like you then," I replied and then asked him about his Ugandan school project where he had been three times before.

"I don't want to talk about it," he said snappily. "If you're so desperate to know, read my blog."

"I'm not obsessed... just asking." "It's all in my blog."

"Do you plan to go again to Africa?"

"Yes, I'm going next year. I've decided and there'll be no discussion... end of. I'm going and that's final."

Wow, what a great way to start a holiday.

Where had the loving man I knew gone? He had dropped a bombshell into my world.

"What do you mean?" I persisted, "What about getting to know the children and spending time with them? It will be their first summer holiday with us as a family."

"It's been settled, no discussion." He pushed aside his plate of baklava to make his point.

Who was this man I was going to adopt two children with? Where were his priorities? I looked away towards the sea, so disappointed, emotional and angry at the same time. We sat at dinner facing a romantic, secluded bay, not talking, and I couldn't stop my eyes from welling up.

Afterwards we headed back to our hotel, walking under the stars, that were shining so brightly over the pretty pastel-coloured houses that lined the waterfront. I felt like I had taken a bullet to my heart. I guess I would just have to handle the children on my own since my husband couldn't be bothered and was more concerned about his next trip to Africa.

During the holiday I was reading Life After Life by Kate Atkinson. I often found the stories, and characters in the books would resonate with me on a higher level, almost telling me something about my own life, or saying something about the people around me. In this story, each character would be born and have several lives, all parallel to the same time frame, but in each story, there was a different outcome of the life that was lived.

Lying alongside my husband on our favourite beach, feeling the hot sun rays, I imagined my life in the future with the children, as I watched a couple with their two young ones playing in the sand. That would be us, our family next summer, I thought to myself, making sandcastles on a beach. My heart beamed with joy and I couldn't contain my feelings of excitement, knowing that I would finally be a mother. I would be caring for our children, two gorgeous little siblings, guiding them, and showing them the love of being in a family.

Then, in another moment my imagination switched, I had a thought, just for a second, what if we didn't get the children and we weren't a family? Oh my God, for a moment I could see a parallel life of us not having the children. I quickly pushed this thought away. I reassured myself that Andy was just sulking and acting this way since he was tired from all the driving around Uganda. He just needed to rest and enjoy our holiday. Life would go as planned. I blotted all the doubts out of my mind. The book was really having an effect on me though.

On the weekend of our return from Greece, we dropped by his parent's house in Surrey to say a quick hello and pick up the car. Andy's dad had Alzheimer's for many years and by this time he was already 96 years old. As soon as we entered the house, Andy started being snappy with his mother, who got upset and left the room. She had said something on his blog, made a comment about him being grumpy. He shouted her down and she refused to speak to him. She took me into the garden and asked if he spoke to me like that. I said no, but that wasn't true. I didn't tell her that his erratic behaviour had reminded me of his father, who had Alzheimer's. He had been angry with me since returning from Africa, and I was tiptoeing around him. I assumed it was just the 'normal stress' of adoption. He had upset his father too, by being impatient when he was only asking him a question.

His mother proceeded to proudly show me where our two children's names were going to be embroidered onto a wall hanging next to the names of their other grandchildren. She was excited about us having the children and being a grandmother twice over again.

On the ride back home, Andy was visibly pissed off. The silence between us was oppressive like hot, stifling air.

Fed up with his moodiness, I asked, "What's wrong... Why did you upset your parents?"

"I hate them." He started to drive erratically along the road, probably just to piss me off.

"Can you please calm down?" I said.

He continued to ignore me. Glancing over, I barely recognised this sweaty, sullen person beside me. "Just remember your dad is very old and unwell, and your mum has to manage him all on her own. It's not easy for her."

He didn't even make eye contact and sulked all the way home.

"Seriously?" I pressed, thinking crikey he's turned into some godawful teenager. He had left his mother in tears and she emailed me before we got home asking what was wrong with him? I said it was difficult for him with his dad dying of Alzheimer's, and he couldn't cope. I thought that was the truth. Looking back now, he was hiding his guilt of his affair with Helen and his mother knew something wasn't right with him. Maybe being his mother, she could see through his charade. She, too, had read the blog since he seemed secretive about his trip. I think his angry reaction was confirmation to her that something was very wrong.

On his return from Uganda two weeks prior, I thought back to when he got his lift with Helen and her husband from the airport. Andy had said he would let me know what time I could meet them at my mother's. He had told me 8 am for their arrival time, but when I got there, he was already there and Helen and Frank had left. He had obviously lied about the time. I found him slumped on my mother's sofa, beaming like a Cheshire cat, so full of himself, sporting a huge beard. He didn't even get up to give me a hug or a kiss, but sat there all smug and knowing. He wasn't as happy to see me as I had imagined. I drove him home and when we got back, he went straight to his study to edit the photos from his trip. He said it was important that he put them all on a CD for Helen. She needed them ASAP and he wanted to deliver them to her the next day.

After a while, I went into his study. I had missed him so much and wanted to connect. Standing beside his desk, I said, "I'd love to see the photos."

"It's all in the blog," he replied irritably. "Can you show me some photos?"

"All the best photos are on the blog."

"I really missed you," I said, touching his shoulder. He flinched. "Did you miss me?"

"Stop being so manipulative."

I couldn't believe how vile he was being. Bursting into tears, I went upstairs. I had felt a sudden jolt to my heart. I had missed him so much and realised I didn't want to be apart from him for such a long time again. That statement should have told me so much more. Instead, I thought maybe I was being too demanding. I was continually making excuses for him: He'd had a long flight and a tough two weeks working in schools out there. While he had been away, I had been getting the house together and planning everything for our future adoptive children. Finding a nursery for Isabella and reading books on parenting.

First thing the next morning, Andy went straight to Helen's to hand over the photos. I went to visit my mother in the same village. Instead of meeting me, he texted to say he was spending the afternoon playing monopoly with Helen's kids. I wish I had gone around there. He was playing happy families while her husband was away on a business trip.

I did meet Helen just one more time. She told us how much she had enjoyed Uganda at her book club. As I sat and told her and another woman about adopting the children and how excited I was, she listened intently. That was the last book club Helen held, and it was the last time I saw her. The other woman in the book club later told me she also noticed there was something different about Helen, as she spoke of her time in Uganda.

My husband wouldn't talk to me about his African trip or even show me the photos. So I took it upon myself to read his bloody blog and it was all there in plain sight: Staying up and watching the stars at 3 am with Helen. He had even put a photo of her and him on his Facebook banner.

So I went straight downstairs and said teasingly, "So 'sitting under the stars with Helen at 3 am is the best day of your life.'"

He looked up at me, fuming.

"What's going on with Helen anyway?" I didn't accuse him of anything since I felt no threat from her, and I never thought he would have an affair. I remember him saying how angry he was about a good friend who had an affair at work and he told me he just couldn't be friends with him anymore. So that reinforced to me that he had strong moral values.

"How dare you say that about Helen?" He started shouting at me. "She sponsored me for the adoption. What would she think of you if I told her what you said? You make me feel sick." He shot out of the house in an angry rampage. He was gaslighting me, as if I had been out of order to even imply that they might have an emotional connection. Only in retrospect, I could see that I had hit a nerve and his reaction said it all.

He returned much later that evening, and I apologised. I had not meant to upset him, it was just an obvious observation from reading his blog, a knee-jerk reaction. Feeling guilty about what I said, I lit the marriage candle.

When he saw what I was doing, he said, "There's no need to light the marriage candle. Just forget it."

"Okay." I blew out the match.

"I've been married to you for five years and we'll be married for another five years." What a weird thing to say, as if I was an object to be kept, not a person to be loved and cherished. I was too exhausted to argue and let it go.

Maybe it was the insecurity of the adoption, the responsibility of having two toddlers in our lives. Either way, I tried to rationalise it, thinking he was probably nervous about the children and had a big workload. I didn't think for a minute he was actually sneaking around and shagging Helen. The fact that he called her his "best friend at school" didn't bother me. I accepted it, working with a school full of women you have to trust your husband. You certainly don't expect him to go off with a married woman with three kids. I knew he was fond of her kids, but this was taking it too far. After all, she had sponsored him for the adoption and had written him a glowing report. Andy insisted that I join Helen's book club, so I could get to know her better. I liked the idea of getting to know more people locally, so I joined. I never thought he would actually go off with her.

My phone was ringing, jolting me back to reality. It was Sara and she was at the train station, ready to be picked up. I jumped out of the bath, got ready, grabbed my keys, phone and handbag and locked the house without even thinking, in a state of pure action. As I drove, I focused on one thought: Sara would bring me back to reality.

At Havant station, I found my sister sitting on a low brick wall. Relief flooded over me at the sight of her face. She was dressed casually in her navy quilted jacket, jeans and trainers.

"You got here quick," I said, hugging her. She held me tightly and I felt for the first time that I was truly awake. When we let go of each other, I could see the worry on her face, perhaps sensing that something was imminent.

"I know. I think the angels were with me. I flew down here—from Leatherhead to Guildford and Guildford to Havant in less than an hour. All the connections just fell into place. Should we go back to yours?"

"I can't face being back there right now."

"Well, let's go to Emsworth," Sara said, referring to a nearby coastal village.

We got into my car and drove, and parking near the pond. It had turned into a bright and sunny day. Light glittered on the surface of the pond as we walked around it to sit on a bench. I began to tell Sara what had happened. Her face looked stricken as I detailed what Andy had said and the cold, emotionless way he had said it. We sat for 20 minutes, overlooking the sea on one side and a tranquil pond on the other. Neither of us could begin to imagine what was going on in Andy's head.

"Maybe he flipped from the stress of the adoption?" I wondered out loud. "Maybe it brought on some kind of mental breakdown."

We'd been told that adopting children was the most stressful time of your life, especially at this point: meeting them for the first time, and beginning to integrate them into your family life. The whole two-year process had been a killer, requiring so much time and effort, and Andy was about to take two weeks off work, which I knew he wasn't happy about. But the adoption agency had insisted he take paternity leave, to give us time to bond with the children. Andy never took a day off work unless he was literally gravely ill.

I couldn't stop thinking about Isabella and Alfie, and what they were going to do when we didn't arrive the next day as we'd promised. I still felt so emotionally connected to them, especially Isabella. I had even sent her my own favourite furry toy, a cream Labrador dog, along with a homemade book. My mother had given me the toy just after my father passed away. He had cancer from asbestosis and died six months after being diagnosed. Soon afterwards, I broke up with Luke, my boyfriend of 14 years, who was bored of dealing with death and, apparently, me. I found out later that he'd been cheating on me with another woman, whom he ended up marrying.

In the wake of that terrible year, I had taken that toy Labrador all around the world with me, to Australia, New Zealand, Argentina and Chile. It was small enough to fit in my pocket when my luggage was full. I loved that little dog and thought it would be nice for Isabella to have it, as it meant something to me. Before giving it to her, I'd photographed the toy dog going to the beach, playing on a swing, and doing other activities I hoped to do with Isabella and Alfie. I'd included the photos in their books I had designed for each of them.

Sam, the foster carer, had been nervous about giving the toy and the book to Isabella. As this was her first fostering job, she was wary of approaching the subject of their 'new' parents. She feared a confused or negative reaction. After all, the siblings had been removed from their biological parents. But they had loved their books. Sam had taken photos of Isabella and Alfie poring over the books and sent them to me. She told me that Isabella had hugged the dog tightly and wouldn't let it out of her sight. She had even sent me a photo of her reaction, cuddling the fluffy toy.

My heart broke at the thought of losing her. "What should I do?" I asked Sara.

The look on my sister's face told me she had no idea. "Let's call Tom," she suggested, referring to our older brother. "Maybe it would help to have a male point of view."

Tom was on the golf course. I overheard Sara telling him over the phone there was a problem with me and to come to meet us in Emsworth. "It's urgent," she said. "Just get down here. We'll tell you when you get here."

While waiting for Tom, we went to a little coffee shop in the village, an old favourite of mine, a breezy, bright white space with a seaside theme. It had an inner courtyard, where we could talk more discreetly. Tired and frazzled, I needed strong black coffee, and my sister was starving. We both ordered avocado on toast with poached eggs. As we ate, I told her what Andy had said, word for word. I replayed the scene matter-of-factly, feeling as though I still wasn't really in my body.

Sara looked down at her plate of poached eggs and shook her head.

"The last thing he'd said was that I would've made a good mother. Was that supposed to make me feel better?"

I saw the shock in my sister's eyes. She was unable to mask her sadness but did her best. As a mother of three children, she was alongside me every step of the way through the adoption and now the collapse of my marriage and adoption. Sara had been training me about how to manage the children, as she had experience as a primary school and a Montessori teacher plus working with children with special needs. She and her husband had even offered to take on our adoptive children in case something happened to both Andy and me. As an adopter, everything must be covered even down to our premature deaths.

At this point, despite my worries and fears about the kids, it hadn't sunk in that I wasn't going to get to adopt them. I couldn't process the fact that my husband could be cruel enough to take them away from me. Never mind the effect it would have on them.

Isabella and Alfie had been put into foster care for a good reason. My husband knew all about their biological parents. Although their local government agency had made every effort to keep the family together, their parents led insecure and dysfunctional lives and couldn't create a safe environment or give their children the stability and nurturing they needed. The agency had spent almost the entire three years of Isabella's life trying to encourage and support the parents through changing their habits and learning the necessary skills. But they couldn't make the changes necessary to meet the local agency's criteria.

Andy knew how much Isabella and Alfie had suffered already, and now he would be making them suffer even more. Why? Because he was selfish and irresponsible? How could he do this to the children and me? I was sure there had to be something very wrong with him.

I left message after message on his mobile, asking him to call. When he didn't, I texted asking him to at least come home from work early to talk. I knew this would be a hard sell since Andy was so rigid about never returning home before 7 pm in the evening.

That afternoon, we met my brother Tom in the car park. He looked bewildered like he was wondering what on earth could be so important he had to leave everything and come down here. "What's up?"

"Well, nothing," I mumbled in breathy rasps, "except Andy woke me up this morning to tell me he had feelings for Helen and doesn't want the children."

Tom looked at me for a long moment. I could tell he was shocked, but seemed to be playing down his reaction so I wouldn't cry. "We need to find a pub. I need a drink."

We went to a nearby pub, the Old House at Home, and found a table in the patio area. It was quiet and the leafy green garden was peaceful—just what we needed. Sara went to the bar to get a glass of wine for Tom. I wanted a glass of wine, too, but I knew alcohol wasn't going to help my situation, and anyway I was driving. The three of us sat hunched around the table in silence. My brother was obviously stressed by the whole thing. He was off to South America in a few days, with his new girlfriend, and he wouldn't be back for at least six months. I'm sure he hated to leave me in such a state.

"Why do you think he's acting like this?" I asked my brother, wanting a bit of insight from a male perspective. "What could Andy possibly be thinking?"

Tom took some big gulps of wine. "I have no idea, but I'll help in any way I can."

As it came up to lunchtime, the pub garden filled with families and couples. Tom was now hungry. I couldn't tell if I was hungry or not, but we all ordered fish and chips. We needed to comfort ourselves. The sun blazed down on us, and time flew by without us noticing as we picked our way through the food. I kept texting and calling Andy.

Finally, he texted back, I can't call. I must speak to the head.

Eventually, Andy agreed to meet me at 5:30 pm. I didn't want to meet him at home and he wasn't keen on my suggestion of meeting in a pub for dinner. So we agreed on a walk.

Tom and Sara went back Laura's house, and I drove alone to nearby Langstone Harbour. Andy and I were set to meet outside the Royal Oak Pub, a place that held many memories for me from when I was a teenager. My friends from college and I used to go there and have parties on a small patch of sandy beach. I was incredibly anxious, yet determined to get to the bottom of what the hell was going on with him. It felt like a life-death situation. It even occurred to me that maybe I could convince Andy to stay with me for now and leave later after I had settled with the children.

As soon as he arrived, we walked side by side along the shore. Andy seemed agitated and impatient, clearly wanting to get this over with. I could see he was rushing to leave. He had long abandoned me and I knew in my heart that it was useless to try to stop him. I thought at the very least, after five years, I deserved some explanation. Stone-faced and avoiding any eye contact, he told me all about how he had been observed in class that day and received the top grade, a distinction with good points.

I thought it was an odd thing to say. He was about to leave his wife, and he had rejected his future children before he even laid eyes on them. What was this man on? He didn't seem connected with reality. I suppose I wasn't anymore either.

"I don't want to hurt you," he murmured quietly.

Like hell you don't, I thought but I did my best to remain calm. After all, Helen had a calm, almost pathetic quality to her voice. I thought that by using that kind of childlike voice myself, I might get better results with him, since apparently that was what he liked now.

"I know you've said Helen is a good teacher, and a good mother and an all-round good person," I began. "But what is it about her that makes you want to be with her?"

"Comfort," he said unexpectedly. I assumed he would say the usual clichéd things, that he had just fallen in love and that it just happened.

"What else?" What was the thing he couldn't get from me, that was so important it led him to destroy our marriage and the chance of a family?

Andy hesitated. "She doesn't ask me about my feelings."

"And I do. Don't I? I ask you all the time."

He nodded without making eye contact.

The triviality of the situation began to hit home for me. The breakdown of our love-sapped marriage was due to the fact that my husband had found 'comfort' with a person who didn't ask him about his feelings. A grown man of 43 years was actually telling me this.

As we talked, I continued using the same low, unthreatening babyish voice. It seemed to be working—he seemed to be telling me the truth. It struck me as absurd that I was using such deliberate tactics to extract information out of this person, my husband, a man I'd thought I knew so well, who I loved and I had thought loved me. The same man who made me hot-water bottles when I was unwell. Who would cuddle up on the sofa and rub my feet for me. The same man who would return home from the weekly shopping, give me a big kiss and a bunch of flowers, just to say how much he loved me. Who loved to create delicious meals for two for Sunday lunch. Who had told me our wedding day was the best day of his life. Obviously, not as great as sitting under the African stars at 3 am with Helen.

"Well, maybe I could stop asking you about your feelings, if that would help?" I suggested half-seriously. "Maybe I could change."

This was, of course, ridiculous. I couldn't change, and he didn't care about me changing either. I could tell he had already made up his mind. He wasn't engaged with me, but off elsewhere, or just going through the motions wanting to get this over with.

The words liar, cheater, sociopath hung on the cusp of my lips, but I remained cool as ever, since shouting and screaming wasn't going to get me the information I needed. More than anything, I was in shock.

I stopped in front of him and made him look me in the eye. "Just do me one favour," I said politely but insistently. "Go and talk to your brother and unravel what's going on in your head." I knew his brother was the only one whom he could talk to, and if anyone could make Andy see sense, it was him.

He agreed, if reluctantly. We walked back to our cars. He looked like a schoolboy hanging his head like he was being forced to do something he didn't really want to do. He rang his brother and said he would drive up to Surrey and see him right then.

Finally, I asked him the question that had been bothering me all day. "When were you going to tell me that you didn't want the children?"

Casually, without betraying any emotion, he said, "Oh... about now." In the weeks that followed, those words played over and over in my head.

"But if you'd only told me five days ago, we could've just not gone to the board, and said we didn't get approval. Instead, we've told everyone."

He just shrugged. "Well, it's done."

Wow, what a kick in the teeth. He clearly didn't give a damn. My husband redefined the perimeters of selfishness. I couldn't comprehend his lack of emotion, his chilling indifference. What had I done to deserve to be with someone so callous, so emotionally stunted?

He got into his car looking like a zombie and headed to his brother's house.

As I sat slumped in my little black Mini, staring blankly, I watched him drive around the corner. I found myself hoping he would make it there in one piece.

I didn't feel I had resolved all the questions in my head. I couldn't process that our marriage was over—so quickly, with no discussion, no counselling, nothing. But the hurt and betrayal went much deeper than the demise of our relationship. It was the end of my dream of being a mother. This was a full-blown crisis. I couldn't believe that there would be no Isabella and Alfie in my life. What must those poor children be thinking, especially three- year-old Isabella, who was old enough to understand that their new parents wouldn't be taking them to their new home.

I headed back to the home Andy and I had shared for the past five years. Before that, it had been my old family home. My mum and dad bought the house in 1979 when I was 12. I'd moved out and up to London at 17. And after my father died in 1999, Mum continued to live there alone until she needed to move out due to health issues.

The house had been on the market for a year when a couple of my siblings suggested that Andy and I should move into it. We lived a few miles away and it seemed like a sensible idea, as it was a four-bedroom home and we planned to have kids. At the time, I had resisted—it felt strange to live in the house I grew up in. But in the end, it seemed too good of a deal to pass up. We decided to totally renovate it so it would be different-looking and feel like our home. I was happy to be back in my lovely neighbourhood, where I had known the people in our street for years. We moved in just after my first miscarriage.

As I turned into our street, it occurred to me that my father would have rolled over in his grave had he known what happened to me that morning in our house. Thankfully, he was cremated, and his ashes had been scattered in the sea long ago.

When I got back, after that pointless meeting with Andy, sitting alone in our living room, I was so sad I could hardly breathe. Everything in my life had gone up in smoke. The man I thought I loved was a cold and callous stranger. The joy, bliss and love I had felt for those two children would never blossom. Just like the woman who had come to speak to the adoption workshop, the loss and heartache would possibly never leave me.

The past month started to flash before my eyes. Andy's behaviour hadn't been quite normal, but then what was normal? Slumped on the sofa, I wasn't sure what to do with myself, my mind was whizzing with thoughts, trying to figure out what Andy was up to. But I still needed hard evidence. Then I recalled a good friend, with whom I had coffee a few weeks previously, oddly she had asked me about Helen. She had seen a photo on Facebook of her and Andy in a London restaurant having African food together. She asked me if I was jealous. I honestly didn't think anything of it and their obsession with everything African at the time didn't ring any alarm bells. Andy even called it his second home. Later I noted Helen was wearing a miniskirt in the photo, a stark contrast from her usual mumsy, flowery dresses.

Over the next few hours, I kept calling Sara, asking for advice, but mostly just needing to talk to someone, needing to feel less alone. I opened a bottle of red wine. After a day like this, I figured I deserved a glass of wine or two. Then a great idea popped into my head. I would text Helen and find out the truth from her. I had her number in my phone from the book club.

Before I could think better of it, I texted Helen, Hi, can you meet me? It's very important. It's about my husband.

Surprisingly, she texted straight back. She said she was needed at home to look after her daughter since her husband was away on business, but that she could meet me the next morning. Surely, she was joking. Even though I'd been the one to suggest it, the idea suddenly seemed preposterous. No way was I actually going to meet my husband's lover, the woman who, along with my smug bastard of a husband, tore apart my life. I texted back, asking if we could talk on the phone instead. She agreed to call me after 10 pm, when her daughter would be asleep.

My adrenaline was pumping. Helen's reaction struck me as

someone who had nothing to hide. Like this was normal, and what she was doing, sneaking around with my husband was reasonable and okay. Only a few months earlier, she had texted to congratulate me on the adoption approval and that she was excited for us. I took a few gulps of wine and sat there in the dark waiting, wondering why she would want to speak to me. Maybe their relationship was completely innocent, and I had jumped to conclusions.

When the phone rang, I was careful to stay calm, asking her politely and directly, "What are you doing with my husband?"

There was a pause and then, in her soft, childlike voice, she said, "Weeeeell..." She drew the word out for a long time, making it sound like it had seven syllables, and then tried to explain why with the usual tired clichés. "You know we were best friends at school. When we went to Africa together, our feelings went deeper—"

"How deep?" I interrupted.

"My feelings went too far."

"So are you leaving your husband and three children?"

"Probably," she said, her tone non-committal.

"Do you realise you're destroying the lives of your three children and your husband, not to mention mine and the lives of our two adoptive children? You're effectively taking away the chances of me being a mother. How would you like it if your kids were suddenly taken away from you?"

There was a pause. "Oh, you must be angry," she said with very little emotion. Angry, is that what I'm feeling?

How could Helen have any idea what I was feeling, when I had no idea myself? I had barely spoken to my husband about what was happening—ten minutes in the morning and twenty minutes after work and he couldn't wait to get away. Yet the life I thought I had evaporated into thin air.

3

The Break up: 1 October 2014

The morning after Andy left felt like the longest day of my life. I woke up, realising that I was on my own now, remembering the miserable details of the day before. Today was the day we were supposed to meet our children. Yet here I was home alone, wrenched with sadness, trying desperately hard not to fall apart. My sister and brother were due over very soon. I hadn't slept much and couldn't think straight. I didn't want a husband that would totally destroy me. My house, full of toys, was all ready to receive our two new children. We had been preparing this for two years.

Andy texted saying he wanted a change of clothes. Well, he can have all his clothes. Selfish bloody bastard. In a frenzy of activity, I quickly packed all his clothes into the suitcases we had, lugged them downstairs and placed in the porch, ready for his collection.

Within ten minutes, he arrived without even ringing the bell or calling me. He grabbed his clothes, filled up his car and was off as if it was planned all along. He politely left a packet of toilet rolls on the porch since we'd run out the day before. He disappeared from my life—never to be seen again. I peeked out of the upstairs window from our bedroom. He didn't want to make a scene. His inability to ring the bell, or call me, made me feel quite odd. Who was this man?

We had agreed to speak that evening, but for all intents and purposes I'd never see my husband again. Why would I want to? What would I say? He didn't even say sorry or have the decency to treat me in a humane way. He told me while half-asleep in bed. I thought he respected women—that's what he said on the adoption forms. The callousness of it, instead of talking to me, he had left me with a pack of toilet rolls and was gone. What a metaphor for an end of a shitty marriage and leaving me to clean up the terrible mess he left behind.

That morning, I had to call the social worker. I had said to Andy that we should do it together and make him call them in front of me. Now I felt I couldn't face him, not after what he had done. I felt destroyed by his heartlessness. I knew I had to do this but still felt nervous. First, I called our social worker, but her phone was engaged. Damn. My heart was beating fast.

So then I rang the children's social worker, Christian, who answered cheerily, "Good morning, how are you on this beautiful day?"

I hesitated a moment on hearing his sunny voice and felt a sense of hope, but then he had no idea about what I was about to say and how it would shatter his day.

"Not great," I began after a pause, "I have some bad news. I'm afraid we won't be able to adopt Isabella and Alfie."

I could feel the shock in his voice. "Um, okay... is everything alright?"

"No, my husband and I have split up. He was having an affair and said that he didn't want the children anymore."

"Wow, that's too bad... I'm sorry to hear that. I need to let people know and sort it out."

In seconds the call was over—I was no longer needed, and the line went dead. I was still holding onto the phone, staring at his name. That's how quickly a life for the three of us could change. Afterwards, I called our social worker, Nikki again, and told her exactly what happened. She said she would make some calls and ring me back.

The deed had been done, the information was sweeping its way into the outer world, and I could no longer call it all back. I'd lost everything, and in doing so I'd lost all sense of myself. I had to get out of the house, to keep on moving. Within two frantic days, my marriage had shattered, and the two gorgeous children, whom I thought would be ours, were gone for good.

After that, I couldn't face staying home in an empty house, with my heart splintering into pieces. Sara, my sister, suggested going to the beach. I got in my little black Mini and drove us down to Southsea Beach. Just as I parked by the golf course, near the Tenth Hole Cafe, Nikki, our social worker, rang. We'd known her for over 14 months of the two-year process. I hadn't warmed to her and found her a little unpredictable. She really liked my husband though. I could feel the sense of camaraderie between them. They had bonded early on since they both worked for the government and cared for children so had an immediate connection. During our first meetings, she had said a few things that I found upsetting, so consequently, I was always on my guard. But after we got approved as adopters, she suddenly became lovely and supportive. I got to know Nikki a little while we went through the adoption. She had two kids herself. She was around 36, but her long greying hair and deeply lined face made her look much older. I guess it was probably from the stresses and strains of her difficult and depressing job as a social worker dealing with neglected, abused and abandoned children.

It was around 11 am when she called back. I can still remember it vividly, sitting in my car, with my sister beside me. Picking up the discomfort in her voice, I immediately asked, "Has Andy called you?" "Yes, he has."

"What did he say?"

"He didn't say a lot," she replied and then asked after an awkward pause, "Did you separate?"

"Guess so." It hadn't dawned on me what my current marital status was, but it was important for her to know to assess the situation for herself. "Could I still adopt the children?"

“Not now.” The words seemed to ricochet a thread of shock throughout my whole body. I anxiously hung on to her every word. I guess I was getting a large shot of my new reality. “I’m sorry you won’t be able to have the kids. Not after what he has done to you. You’ll be in no fit state.”

No fit state, I thought, is she talking about me? How could she possibly know what state I would be in? In hindsight, she had the experience of this kind of thing before.

After it all started to slowly sink in, I asked, “So what’s the procedure now?”

“There isn’t one. I’ve called into the office to ask my boss, but he wasn’t in.” I was stunned. They seemed to have a procedure for everything else. She continued, as it was the day before the placement week, there was nothing in place to deal with a breakdown in the adoption process at this stage. She proceeded to tell me she knew exactly what my husband was, “a fantasist.”

Oh, she knows everything about him too, and what he is. I realised in that moment that I didn’t know who my husband was. Still, in massive shock, I had this notion that maybe Andy was mentally ill. He had been acting odd lately. Anyone who would do this to those sweet, beautiful little kids who already had a rough start in life, was surely mentally unstable. Everyone knew we were getting these children, our families, our friends, and everyone we met in our day-to-day lives.

I was shocked to hear from Nikki, that there was no special procedure, so I asked her what I should do. She rattled off a long list of things, and I wrote them down as she spoke. I had been a project manager in a previous life, working on glossy women’s magazines like Marie Claire, InStyle and House and Garden, so I was used to adapting to changing situations and dramatic people. I was good at keeping calm in a crisis.

I calmly wrote down all her suggestions:

1. Write a letter to the children to say why you can’t be their parent.

2. Write a letter withdrawing from the adoption process immediately.

3. DESTROY everything, photos, data, confidential information etc.

4. Your husband will be sued as he is an 'irresponsible adult' in the care of children.

This last bit was because of his position as an assistant head teacher in a primary school, where he was responsible for the welfare of children.

Rightfully, as a social worker, Nikki seemed furious with the situation. But I also felt her anger towards me. It was hardly my fault that my husband was shagging his co-worker and pulling out of the adoption at the eleventh hour. I sat in my car, shell-shocked and lost for words, with my loyal sister beside me, listening to every word. She could hear the fury in Nikki's voice. And afterwards, on my iPhone I took notes, so I didn't forget anything. The words she spoke stayed imprinted on my mind, for days and weeks to come. I was stunned. I couldn't comprehend how my social worker knew everything, that she had decided just there and then, without asking anyone, that I could no longer have my children, and that my husband was a fantasist. How did she know so much? How could I have been so much in the dark?

This news left me devastated. My heart rate was already beating at a rate of knots. I couldn't believe what I was hearing. That, or I didn't want to be hearing this. What was happening to me, my life, my husband, and my adopted children? I had prepared for two long exhausting years and now it was all over in a flash.

No empathy or understanding for my sudden predicament. No sympathetic words. Nothing. I couldn't believe it. Why was all this suddenly my fault? My husband will be sued. Weirdly, I felt worried for him too. His life would be ruined, his career and probably his reputation if they took him to court over this.

After the call, I sat there, stricken and dazed, clutching my phone as though it was a security blanket. Sara, who was as shaken as me, glanced over. "Come on," she said softly, opening the car door, "We need to get out, go for a walk and get some sea air."

Our father had his ashes scattered on Southsea Beach, and we walked along the shore wanting to be close to him. My sister had been particularly close to him. I loved him, but as the youngest sibling, I hadn't spent as much time with him as she had. I prayed to my dad that he would help me through this awfulness. Alone at night, I felt he was in some way protecting me since I was living in our old family home.

This was definitely not the happy ending I had planned for—no one could've planned for this agonising ending let alone imagined it. All that effort and I was left with nothing. An empty nest and eventually I would lose my house too.

Now, somehow, I had to pull myself together to tell my mother and my other sisters what has happened. Sara and I got back in my Mini, 'Maurice', as I named the car when I bought it. We drove to my sister Laura's house, in a small village, outside of Petersfield, in Hampshire. It was a good 40-minute drive and we prepared ourselves to tell our family. I drove in silence, there was nothing to say. I knew what I had to do. My family suspected something was up but didn't quite know what. It was odd, my sister Kathy happened to be over from abroad, Tom had stayed over from yesterday's visit, and Sara had stayed too. This was more than a bit unusual. The only one of my five siblings who wasn't there was my brother Tony in Australia. A bit of a loner, Tony moved there in his 20s and I had rarely heard from him since. Although we had spoken on the phone, the day after Andy had left. I was unable to sleep, and I needed someone to talk to and he had listened to my story.

4

Bad Luck Blues

My sister Laura lived in a lovely old turn-of-the-century farmhouse, which had been converted so our mother could have a self-contained home there too. When we arrived, their large Labrador Monty, a blur of golden blonde fur and long legs, came bounding out to greet us, jumping for joy and wagging his tail excitedly.

Steeling myself, I worried about having to tearfully explain to our 81-year-old mother that my lying, cheating husband had just run off with another woman, that he didn't want our adopted children and left me to deal with the wreckage. As soon as Sara and I walked through the back door into the kitchen, where our two older sisters Laura and Kathy were sitting around the large kitchen table chatting, I said hello and explained that I had to go and speak to Mum. They looked up at me slightly confused by my abruptness.

I had already decided I had to tell my mum first since I sensed she knew something was going on. I guess it's a mother's intuition—she could feel there was something different than what everyone was seeing on the surface. I strode into Mum's kitchen where she was standing by the sink and my brother Tom walked over and stood with her protectively. You never know how people are going to react to shocking news.

She took one look at me and said angrily, "Where is he?"

She stared straight into my eyes, so I couldn't lie. I hadn't seen my mother like this since I was a teenager, when I misbehaved or had done something wrong.

"He's not here," I said defensively. "I think maybe you should sit down."

"I don't want to sit down." The look of thunder on my mother's face was like a volcano about to erupt. Although she's 81, she doesn't count herself as being very old.

As the three of us, Mum, Sara and I sat down around her kitchen table, I said, "He doesn't want me or the children. He woke me up and told me that he has feelings for Helen at his school. But I'm okay... guess I have to be." My mind was working on overdrive, wanting to reassure my mother.

Tom had hung around for 24 hours at Mum's, since he was off on a long round-the- world trip with his girlfriend for many months. I asked Tom to tell my other two sisters who were sitting in Laura's kitchen drinking tea. When they both came and hugged me, I felt numb, not knowing what else to say. Kathy would be going back to Nepal a few days later. Only the day before she and I had driven two hours to IKEA to get Alfie a cot. Even though he was 18 months old, the social worker and carer felt he still needed one and that it would help him settle into his new home with us.

Kathy, my second oldest sister after Laura, blonde and green-eyed, looked very different from our other siblings. Very social and free-spirited, she loved travelling like me. She was a counsellor and volunteered in countries around the world, including Tanzania, Vietnam and India. Since she was going to be in Nepal soon, it meant I could talk to her at night time, when in the UK, everyone except me and other insomniacs, are awake. I needed some night-time reassurance as it was when I suffered the most. The pain, fear and grief came alive at night. I guess in truth I needed sedating.

After speaking to my sisters, I went back and saw my Mum in her lounge, with Monty, the family dog, sitting at her knees. I bent down and hugged him. He was always by Mum's side, caring for her and keeping her company. He looked sad, a dog's eyes never lie—he had picked up on the heightened emotions in the room. I cuddled him and told him he was a good boy. I had an affinity with him and felt he was trying to tell me something. Then I remembered that he had lost all his pups. Poor Monty had been a breeding dog and lived a hard life in a kennel on a farm, until he was adopted by my sister Laura's family. We all came to love him immensely, even people who weren't keen on dogs liked Monty, he was such a gentle, sensitive soul. He didn't rush up to strangers like a mad over-excitable dog. He was a plush ball of shimmering pale-gold fur, with big, soulful brown eyes.

Watching him, I felt that he was trying to show me he understood my sadness. He was snuggling around a group of Labrador puppy ornaments that my mum had around her fireplace, his head bowed, looking at them mournfully. I'd never seen him do this before. He seemed to know that like him, I had lost something too.

Looking up, I saw a photo my mother had of our future adoptive children on the mantelpiece. Without thinking, I blurted out, "That has to be destroyed. The social worker had said I have to destroy everything."

Later that evening, returning to mine, Sara and I were drained and ready for dinner. I didn't have much food in the house, and we were too exhausted to cook anyway. Thankfully she had made lots of home-cooked vegetarian ready-made dishes. She was thoughtfully trying to help me out for the upcoming busy adoption period. I had put them all in my freezer, ready for when the kids arrived. We heated up a couple of home-made Indian dishes my sister had lovingly made.

As we sat in the dining room, eating in silence, Sara jumped up and said, "Right, where is that bloody marriage candle? We need to burn that right now."

It was there in the corner of the room. My sister grabbed it and set it alight. There were three wicks, and it was going to take some time to burn since it was a giant candle. She got to work on it, the ceremony had begun. The light was going out on this marriage.

My husband insisted on getting married in a Catholic church. We had both been brought up as Catholics. I had lapsed since leaving school, but he liked to go at Christmas and special occasions. Although I didn't want to get married in a church, I went along with it since it meant so much to him. In fact, weirdly, he had also insisted on getting married at the age of 38 like his father had. A good omen, I had thought at the time, but a bit of a stick-in-the-mud too. I would've preferred getting married alone and spontaneously, and then having a small, intimate party for friends and family. Not waiting over a year at our age, especially since we wanted to have children.

The whole church thing troubled me. I had always admired the Dalai Lama and preferred the Buddhist philosophy. I felt Catholicism was full of hypocrisy and deceit—not to mention all the corruption and paedophile priests. Religion in itself is not all bad. There are some good elements in all religions, the sense of community, kindness and it helps some people make sense of their lives. But by the time I was 16, I had made my choice not to go to church. The only time I went was to attend a funeral. So, when we eventually agreed to get married in a church, we scouted around for the right one, which we found locally, along with a lovely Irish-Canadian priest. Father Joe, whose homilies were interesting, relating to current issues, he had more of a modern approach to life. We started to go to the local church, and I had a bit of an issue. I was fine until I got halfway through a mass, and then I'd start to cry. We tried lots of different churches, masses without music, as I thought maybe the songs made me teary. I guess it reminded me of all the funerals I had been to. After my father's funeral in 1999, there seemed to be a steady stream of deaths that year. Part of me sensed it might have been a sign that my marriage wasn't going to bode well.

As part of the mass, we had to have a marriage candle, so when you have special occasions or have an argument you can light it, resolve the issue, and make up. To help guarantee a long marriage, I bought the biggest candle I could find. At 30cm high and 10cm wide, it was a whopper. Funnily enough, during our marriage, Andy didn't like me to light it, so it just sat there collecting dust. Only a month earlier, I had lit it after we had a row about Helen.

The monstrous candle, white and decorated in a garland of small pink hearts connected with wire, was going to take some burning. Sara and I opened a bottle of sparkling wine too. We needed a drink to cope with the awfulness of the day. I had made the decision to take off my wedding bands, my marriage was over with less than an hour of discussion. It had been like a burning bush, over in moment and only the charred embers remained. One being that bloody candle. Sara had lit the three wicks. It was a moment of liberation. It took hours to burn, and my sister had wax running across the table as she stabbed it, trying to get it to melt quickly. The wax ran across the cheap, ugly rectangular table, one of the few items my husband had brought to the marriage before we met.

In a mad moment, I decided I'd call him one last time and see what he had to say for himself. I put my phone on speaker, by the hatch between the lounge and kitchen so Sara could hear him too. I felt I needed a witness to the madness that was becoming my life. Standing in the kitchen, I called his phone, and it rang several times before he answered it. I said hello and he appeared quiet and distant. All he said was "why did you put all my clothes in the porch? I only wanted a change of clothing?"

I didn't have a chance to answer him, before he spluttered angrily, "And why did you befriend Frank on Facebook?"

"Well, you're friends with Helen. Why can't I be friends with Frank?" "What have you said to him?"

"Nothing." I hadn't spoken to Frank by that point, but thought I would probably contact him to find out what he knew about their affair.

How odd, I thought, Andy was some strange foreigner that had been in my life and that had disappeared without a trace.

I realised the man I married no longer existed. Maybe he never really existed. They say you project what you want in a relationship. Maybe I had idealised and created him in my mind. In actual fact, he turned out to be a fake, a cardboard cut-out of a man living a lie.

In that angry, stilted phone conversation, with lots of silences, he said quietly, "Look, I don't have anything more to say. I'm tired and want to go to bed."

He said nothing about our marriage or the two children we had just rejected the day before. He didn't even have the decency to apologise. What a pathetic, infantile creature. He had created this god-awful mess by not facing up to his sudden change of heart.

All I knew was what my husband had told me and he was a stunning liar. This was confirmed by Frank, Helen's husband, a month later when he told me he had confronted him at the local country park, on the Sunday before our break up. He'd warned Andy to "stay away from my wife."

Andy, on the other hand, had told me that morning when he shook me awake, that Frank was going to tell the head, and that he didn't want him to teach his son. Weeks later, when I spoke to Frank, he denied it and said he would never do such a thing, to hurt his son by removing him from his school class. Sometimes I am so stupidly gullible.

Sara and I continued drinking, as the candle slowly melted into an ugly puddle of wax. It became a sacred ceremony to the ending of my five-year marriage. It was over in an instant, a new life begins tomorrow.

5

The Aftermath

The first week of October 2014, as I was coming to terms with everything, the days continued, thankfully still warm and sunny. I drove my mother and sister down to the beach for lunch. My family loved being by the sea since we had grown up by it. Again, we went to Southsea to a fab new restaurant right on the beach. This was a novelty for us, as most of the beachfront cafés were pretty soulless and shabby. This new one was different, and we ate a lovely lunch of fish and chips, one of my dad's favourites. I felt the need to reassure my mother that I would be okay. I wasn't fully in my body, I was kind of floating in another reality but still functioning.

When we were children, Mum would often take us to the beach after school with a picnic and take as many of our friends as we could squeeze in her tiny VW Beetle. My parents had been born in the north of England and had lived by the seaside, so it had been an important element in their lives. The simple carefree joy of spending time by the water, playing and swimming would never leave me. I really missed the sea when I lived in London for over 20 years. I'd often go home at weekends. In recent times I had returned to the south coast to live and so the sea had once again become a part of my life.

This particular beach had a special significance and connection for my family. After my dad died, we scattered his ashes at sea, at a spot a little further from the café. A part of him was sailing around the world, and a part of him was everywhere we went around the world. Dad had spent many years driving down to this beach and watching the waves, as it reminded him of his childhood in Hartlepool, a northern coastal town where my parents were both from.

I thought of myself as an optimistic person. I knew it was going to be tough, but somehow I knew I would be fine. I'd tell myself my life wasn't meant to be that way. But at night, the tears would come. Sleep was impossible as my body was in an enormous amount of pain. I was bleeding heavily; this wasn't my usual type of period. My heart shuddered in a way I'd never experienced before. At the time, I thought I was dying.

During the adoption process and for over two years, I had been using Vedic mantras and singing them was calming and took me to a place of peace. During the sleepless nights, I listened to my mantra and sang along. They gave me the strength to get through the night. The mantra I had chosen was called Om Namo Bhagavate Vasudevaya, it was for Vishnu and Krishna. It's known as a mukti mantra, or 'the liberator', a spiritual formula to attain freedom. It has a double meaning: it can be used to welcome your spiritual children into your life or as a way of overcoming obstacles. I had originally chosen the mantra since I had wanted to have children. As I lay awake grieving, I sang to cope with the deep feeling of loss for the children that I would no longer meet and have in my life.

The nights were long. At times, lying awake, I felt I was going to have a heart attack. It got to the point that I would sing the mantra throughout the whole night repeatedly. It kept me in the present and alive. I could anchor my mind onto the mantra. It was odd, during the day I managed to function normally, but at night I felt I was dying over and over again.

Thankfully, I lived in a detached house and I didn't disturb the neighbours with my nightly singing. Some evenings, I'd call Sara, who was sleeping in the next room and she would come and sit with me. I was frightened of what was going on with my body, the shaking, and the clattering of my heart.

One night I wrote a letter saying I didn't want to be resuscitated or have any medical intervention should my body give up on me. I know, in retrospect, it sounds dramatic, but I truly thought I was dying. Looking back now, it was a massive mistake. I couldn't trust organisations because of what had happened and, after the adoption fell through, I had no support from the social worker. Aside from my sister Sara, I couldn't trust anyone. I could feel that she felt my pain. Sara and I, being the youngest of six, shared a bedroom and had a close connection since early childhood. Although Sara was only four years older, she was very sensitive and emotional and more of the baby in the family. We even looked similar, petite, brown-eyed with dark-brown hair, although she had more delicate and daintier features. It was through this deep connection we had, that she was able to transmit her energy to me and vice versa. I had never done this energy exchange before, but it felt natural. As she held my hands, I could feel her energy enter my body and it gave me more power to go on. She would then go back to her room to lie down as she was drained and exhausted.

As I lay there falling apart, I had half-expected the adoption agency to send someone to see if I was okay. All I had was an answerphone message from my social worker, saying, "Sorry if I seemed a bit harsh with you yesterday. Take your time and let me know if you want to discuss anything." Her voice sounded remorseful and uncomfortable. She was supposed to be supporting us through this stressful adoption. How could she help me after she told me to destroy everything? She showed no empathy or compassion. Instead, she had been angry with me, as if I knew what was going on. Surely if anyone would have known the dreadful effect this was going to have on me, she would have reached out in person. I suppose she was concerned about the consequences and long-term impact it could have on her career as a social worker. She had a husband and two small children to manage, alongside a stressful full-on job.

Sara said to me she could see I was in so much pain it was like I was physically giving birth to these children and/or miscarrying them. I was bleeding for ten days afterwards. I wasn't sleeping through the night and was scared when I woke up. I would be woken up by a jolt of electricity in my body. I felt scared of sleeping in my bed where it had all happened that morning. I feared the shadows of the night. Everything around me felt so bleak.

During the day, I was whizzing around in my Mini, taking Sara and Mum everywhere. Kathy was worried and said that I shouldn't be driving in my mental state. Sara told her that "Alice has more energy than all of us". I couldn't see it then, but I was burning myself out. Not much sleep. Too much fear. I was living in a parallel universe, a bit like when Dad was dying, and my life was on hold. I started thinking about what else my husband might be doing. I thought it was ironic how he rejected our adoptive children without warning, yet was running off to help children halfway across the world in Africa at every chance he got.

After five days, Sara couldn't cope with me any longer. She was beginning to irritate me too, as I was working at full-speed-ahead mode and she was trying to keep up. We hadn't fallen out, but I knew I must have been exasperating. My mind was all over the place, and I was being short-tempered with her. I didn't know then that my blood pressure was sky high and I needed proper rest. I could feel the adrenaline pumping around my body. I spoke fast and was impatient, my mind was clouded, but somehow I was holding it together. I knew my life was a huge mess and I had to pull myself from the ruins and figure it out.

Exhausted and burnt out, Sara wanted to go home to her husband and three kids. She asked a close family friend to help. One afternoon Marcus arrived smiling and happy to see us. A tall, friendly guy with grey hair and piercing blue eyes, he had been a family friend since I was a child. He was ten years older than me, so kind of like an older brother. The last time I saw him was at my wedding in 2009. When I was a child, we used to call him Mr Obridge, a character from a British television show. As a teenager, he used to work at the local butcher's and delivered our weekly meat order. He would often bring us chewy milk-bottle sweets too. We started calling him Mr Obridge because once when I was ill, he helped my mother give me my medicine.

Marcus and his wife Stephanie had been childhood sweethearts. My family had known his family through going to the same Catholic church and community events over the years. Marcus's mother worked at the school as a secretary. My family liked him a lot and he and Stephanie had a strong bond with my dad when he was alive. They had all been on the Catholic committee together, at the local Catholic social club, a place where you could play skittles, bingo, hold events and socialise. Every Friday there were discos at the community hall and my friends, and I would go and dance the evening away. We once held a surprise party for my father's 60th birthday and Sara had her wedding reception there back in the 80s. At the time it was very uncool to be a bridesmaid, but I did it for my sister, wearing an emerald coloured taffeta dress, with big puffy sleeves.

When Marcus showed up at the house, Sara went to the town centre to see who had put up the FOR SALE sign behind our back fence, indicating that our house was on the market. We'd seen the sign when we returned the night before and it freaked us both out. It was some kind of premonition that the house would be sold now that my marriage was over. I could imagine this was Andy's doing, probably wanting to cash out to finance his new life with Helen. As we entered the house from the back door, it felt strange and had an eerie feel to it. Sara and I were spooked. We didn't say anything to each other, but we both felt it and went about the house lighting candles to raise the vibration of the place. Before long, we forgot about it. We agreed it felt like someone had been in the house while we were away. Neither of us had ever experienced anything paranormal, but had picked up on the weird strong energy in the house.

Marcus was organised and there was no messing with him. He sat me down like my dad would've done and slowed my pace of conversation. After telling me what he could do for me, he asked, "Do you want my help?"

I was confused by this question. "Yes, of course."

"Okay, you need to get two notebooks and write everything down that happened, date it, and create evidence. It's all about the evidence. Let's start with your finances. Do you have a joint-bank account?"

"Yes, I added Andy to my account, so that he could get the free travel insurance and other benefits."

"You need to call the bank to restrict his access to your joint account."

Then, Marcus, asked me to call the head of my husband's school to find out if he was still working there. He wanted to know how the head had been supporting Andy during the adoption process. I asked the questions, he said, "I asked him about his feelings." When I asked if Andy had been assessed in class, he replied he hadn't fully assessed it yet, but it was "probably a good with outstanding features." I know how trivial this may seem, but aside from my husband telling me our marriage was over, on the same day, he boasted about getting an outstanding grade for his teaching. So, that morning before work, he dumped his wife, rejected his adoptive children, and then got an outstanding lesson observation in the afternoon. Who on earth had I married?

Marcus persuaded me to call Helen's husband to try and establish what was going on between his wife and my husband since we needed evidence. I called Frank and he told me he wasn't going to speak to the head that day or any day. Although he did tell me that he found inappropriate text messages on his wife's phone, Good morning, my beautiful gorgeous, attractive girl. I wrote it down, so

I wouldn't forget it. He confided that he'd been reading their text and Facebook conversations for over five weeks. While I had been preparing myself for getting the house ready for the children, my husband had been texting and meeting up with his lover. I wrote and recorded all the conversations in my new pink book. It was an unnerving fact-finding mission. A useful tool as primary evidence so I could remember what was said and what actions I took. Each day I would practically forget what had happened the previous day, so it was useful. After our discussions, Marcus agreed to help me and he would go home and bring his wife Stephanie back with him and we would take it from there.

I recall having ISABELLA and ALFIE in little wooden letters on my kitchen windowsill, which my sister Kathy had brought for them. Beside them, was my little Balinese stone Buddha, a shalom monk. I had candles and/or electric night lights lit all day and night as a vigil for the children that I had loved and lost. I had to keep the light shining. I was scared of the dark and sleeping in the marital bed, where it had all started that morning. Every day, during the first week, I would wake up to the realisation that I was now alone.

6

Dorset Daze

The second week after Andy left, Sara's husband Dan came to collect her. He didn't want to come into the house and see me and insisted on picking up my sister from around the corner or somewhere nearby. It seemed odd to me. In the end, he came into the house. I was sitting in the lounge and he flopped down on the sofa opposite. I told him what had happened, and he looked uncomfortable. Seeing the faces of shocked people wasn't helping me, as they reflected back what had happened to me and it made me feel worse. It made me realise how bad things were. I wanted to help everyone else around me cope and I had forgotten I had to help myself first.

How the hell had I gotten myself into this weird situation? It had happened so quickly, having the rug pulled from underneath me. If I had been given sufficient warning, I'm sure I would've coped with the outcome in a more sensible manner. I know I would never have wanted to live with someone who didn't love me, and certainly not bring two children into our lives if we hadn't agreed wholeheartedly.

On a daily basis I would ask Sara if this was really happening? She would say, "Do you have your children? Do you have your husband?" I'd reply, "No." And she'd say, "Well then. It's true." I knew that much was true, but I felt some deep and inexplicable connection to those children, whom I hadn't even met. The seed of love and becoming their mother had already grown within me.

The evening Sara left with Dan back to their normal life, Marcus returned with his wife Stephanie. They looked around the house and had to decide where they would be sleeping.

The only option was to sleep in the children's rooms. Marcus scouted out the rooms, filled with all the toys and objects I had created for their cute little rooms. In Alfie's room, Marcus found a beautifully handcrafted old wooden trunk he had made for me when I was a child. I watched him admire his craftsmanship from long ago, it was as if his mind was going through the process of remembering making them for us. I think my mother had asked him to make one for me and Sara. It was too heavy to lug around, but I kept all my doll's clothes and toys in it. My mother used to make gorgeously sown dresses for our dolls. I could see he felt moved by being reunited with the wooden box and being able to spot his workmanship 40 years later.

Marcus had helped my parents move into this house back in 1985. The days when you used to bring your carpet and refit it in your new home. He had refitted our lounge carpet for us. There was a lot of history between our families. My dad had been like a surrogate father figure to him. His father was a part-time magician among other things and, as a five-year-old, I had been a bunny in his magic show, popping out of a set and doing bunny hops.

That night, Marcus slept in Alfie's room while Stephanie slept in Isabella's. They couldn't bear being in the house filled with the children's things, without any children. Instead, Marcus thought I needed a change of scenery, and a break in Dorset where they lived would lift my spirits.

Before setting off, my sister Laura came over and suggested that I pack a bag. In my frenzied state, I started packing up the whole house. I was very sensitive to what anyone said and took things literally. Marcus politely told me I couldn't take everything but just a few essentials for a short break away.

We drove down to Dorset and it was already dark when we

arrived at their house. I couldn't remember the name of their small village, so I renamed it 'Wa Wa land'. Marcus had already set the ground rules with me: to sleep well, eat well, do the work, then play— meaning going for leisurely walks in the woods and getting some fresh air, exercise and rest. Of course, this also involved writing everything down as evidence. I had several books I wrote in, and I became obsessed with buying stationery during this time, to fill up with my thoughts and fears.

The first day I woke up, with the sun streaming through the window, I was in this strange place I had never been before. I wandered around and found myself in the kitchen. I could feel the energy of their lovely home with a view of the rolling green fields beyond. Out of the kitchen windows, you could see a large field with cows in it. Well, so Marcus told me. The expanse of grass felt relaxing and calming to look at. He said that the cows came in so close they could watch the television. During my stay, I was constantly on the lookout for cows in the back garden area but never saw any.

The countryside was relaxing. I sat down at the round farmhouse table and Marcus asked me what I wanted for breakfast.

"An egg please," I said, watching him flapping around the kitchen. I chatted away with him, even though he had his back turned to me while cooking. I had forgotten he was deaf, in not one, but both ears, and he wasn't wearing his hearing aid.

I later emailed Sara, thinking he was taking the piss, how hard was it to make an egg? He was supposed to be looking after me and he could barely make an egg. Eventually, I got my egg, with one piece of untoasted bread.

At the time, I thought Marcus was some kind of psychologist, who was going to sort out my head. I'd spotted various psychology books on his bookshelves, but he told me they belonged to his daughters. I felt sort of safe in his hands. He was there for me and seemed keen to help me out of this deep, dark hole.

After breakfast, Marcus told me he was going out to do a few jobs locally. He was involved in a campaign to stop the building of wind turbines in Dorset. There were many signs around the village, saying NO GIANT WIND TURBINES AROUND HERE, which said in a Dorset accent sounds right, but not any other accent. It just didn't roll off the tongue. We had many laughs about this. "When pronounced in a Dorset accent, 'Nooo giiii ant wind tuurrrbines round 'ere". But 'no giant wind turbines around here' said in a southern English accent sounded strange and made me laugh. It wasn't a joking matter, but a real issue for the local community fighting for their landscape and their health. Marcus wore hearing aids, and the turbines would potentially interfere with them.

As we drove around the countryside stopping at these homemade signs, he got out an electric saw and started chopping down the hedges to make the signs more visible.

"Why are you cutting the hedges?" I shouted but he couldn't hear me over the buzz of the chainsaw. I couldn't believe it. Being hypersensitive to everything around me especially sound, I immediately slipped on my headphones to listen to my mantras. Marcus was up a ladder in the middle of a narrow winding lane. Worried he might get run over, I stood in the road and started dancing around to distract myself from the sound. I ended up dancing in a field of rain-soaked green grass, listening to my calming music.

Sara had warned Marcus that I sang my mantras all night long, but since he was a bit deaf, he'd never heard me. It kept me distracted and alive at night. I'd go off into another world, wherever the music took me. At the same time, I was petrified of hearing the sound of his electric saw again and fearing Marcus would fall, so I steadied the bottom of the ladder. I thought this man was crazy. He kept doing this for what seemed like ages. I counted at least eight times we stopped, and he got out of his car to cut down bushes, so that the signs could be seen clearly. Not sure what he would do next, I just went with the flow.

At one point, I glimpsed a cute cottage with a red door with a 'For Sale' sign and snapped a picture of it. In that moment, I felt happy and free of everything. Glancing down at my feet, my Converse were soaked from dancing in the wet grass.

"Why didn't you tell me to wear my wellies, my feet are wet now?" I moaned to Marcus.

"I don't want the farmers to know what I'm doing."

Then we headed back to his house and swapped cars. I was confused by this odd behaviour, but I went along with it and changed my clothes and shoes. This whole campaign added another surreal aspect to my whole stay. The fact that when he went around clipping hedges and we were also hiding from the farmers, whom I thought were the baddies, underpinned my heightened state of unreality.

It was mid-afternoon and we hadn't had lunch yet. With my mind doing overtime, I got exhausted quite quickly. Marcus drove to Lulworth Cove, a little limestone village, and told me about a man known locally as 'Chris the hippy', who painted stones and shells. We walked down the hill to the water's edge. When we reached the cove, the water was swirling in all directions. It made me feel disoriented and dizzy. I couldn't bear it any longer, so I looked away in the opposite direction inland.

As we turned around, there he was, Chris, his long, dark, silver-flecked hair in a ponytail, quietly painting stones. Perched on a rock by the cove, his body merged with the grassy hillside behind him, he was so still you could easily miss him. We went over to say hello. I'd always loved pebbles and was fascinated by the brightly coloured stones. Apparently, Chris lived in a mansion he inherited on top of the hill with his girlfriend and came down to the beach every day to paint.

Fascinated by this character, with his long, silvery hair and beard, sitting there alone painting, I asked, "So how long have you been painting stones at the cove?"

"Oh, about 25 years," he said, in his thick Dorset accent.

"Ah, I see," Marcus and I both said, as if we couldn't believe this man was real. His shirt, jeans and hands were splattered in different coloured paint. He sat like a stiff ornament, opposite the whirling water in front of the cove. His calming presence brought tranquillity to my busy mind. He was otherworldly like how I imagined a leprechaun to be.

His beautiful stones, painted with animals, insects, flowers, miniature landscapes and inscribed with poems, were unique and each told a story. My eye was drawn to a seascape of Chesil Beach, a soothing wash of blue sky and blue sea.

"I'll take this one," I said, looking at it more closely. The writing was very small but beautifully formed. It was a passage from an Emily Dickinson poem: An hour is a sea / Between a few and me / With them would harbor be! Not quite sure what it meant, I asked Chris.

"It means short duration personal saviour " When he read it out loud, I understand it completely.

"How did you know?" I was bowled over. I knew this terrible time was going to be a short and only temporary experience, but how on earth did this stranger know about me? I had chosen a stone that reflected my current situation. I was so excited by this revelation by Chris that I thought he must be a sage. I asked him to inscribe my stone on the back: Alice Readman, 7th October 2014. It was a way of reclaiming my original maiden name.

I asked Marcus to choose a stone and one for Stephanie too. Hers had a pink lotus flower and said something like how lotus grows in mud to become the most beautiful of all flowers. For himself, Marcus chose one with this poem on it: Whether the weather be cold, or whether the weather be hot, we'll weather the weather. Whatever the weather, whether we like it or not.

Funnily enough, my granddad Tierney used to say this rhyme

to us as children. I was buzzing with excitement from this mystical encounter with Chris.

I had found my personal saviours in my life, Marcus and Stephanie. They were saving me from the hell I was going through by looking after me in Dorset when I had nowhere to go. They listened and gave me a safe space to sleep. I had thought I was on the way up and everything would be okay once I caught up with some sleep and rested.

I felt the universe had come to my rescue. Little did I know then what was going to come up for me later.

7

My Week in Dorset

The next morning when I went down to the kitchen, Marcus was scribbling a note saying that he was going out. Panicked, I caught him on his way out the door and said,

"You can't leave me alone in this house. I don't feel safe here."

He seemed surprised. "I'm just popping out to the shop. We're out of eggs, and the kettle's broken."

"Well, I don't want to stay here alone." I quickly slipped on my Converse so he couldn't say no.

When we got to Blandford, a nearby town, Marcus said I might like to go into a shop while he queued for the kettle. I browsed around, and it was full of things that I thought since I was on a sort of holiday, would make nice presents. I found some gorgeously scented handmade soap for my sisters and friends, and some Indian sandalwood soap for the boys. Although I didn't have any money on me. My brother Tom had lent me some cash, so I had some somewhere. I had developed this sudden phobia of money. I felt it was evil and dirty and couldn't bear to touch it. My family had arranged for my money to go in a tin box with a picture of an owl on it and Marcus looked after it for me.

The lovely Indian lady who owned the shop was so sweet. While I was in the shop, I had sort of turned into someone else. I told the woman her business would be more prosperous if she opened another shop. I felt I was having some spiritual insight or message for her. After leaving the shop, I saw another homeware boutique next door with Christmas decorations shaped like eggs but no ordinary ones, they were beautifully hand-painted. I popped inside and I saw one with a blue ribbon and another with a pink one. They represented my children, the ones I couldn't have, but I could hang a decoration on my Christmas tree in memory of them instead I thought. I found another one of two owls. It reminded me of my dad and how we used to say he looked like an owl. I felt my dad had asked Marcus and Stephanie to look after me, so I could get through this terrible temporary experience.

By this point, I was starving and feeling a bit faint. Marcus and I decided we were going to skip breakfast and go straight for lunch and off on another adventure in his car. This time we went to Weymouth and Portland. As we drove up a big hill overlooking Chesil Beach, Marcus pointed out the beautiful view coming up as he drove. Weirdly, I was too scared to look at it. Pulling into the hotel car park at the top of the hill, I suddenly had a vision of my husband in the hotel with another woman. I panicked and told Marcus to drive on, and he sped out of the car park in an instant. All this exposure to these new places was making me feel overwhelmed again.

We ended up in Portland where there happened to be a restaurant called the Lobster Pot, the same name as the Catholic social club my dad and Marcus had helped to build and run many years ago back in the 80s, although it no longer existed. By this time, it was four o'clock and we needed to eat.

When we walked into the restaurant it was packed. There were too many people for my liking, which made me feel vulnerable and sensitive to the energies of the other people in the huge wide-open space. I talked non-stop to Marcus and tried to distract myself. He spoke about my dad and the happy days they had shared at the Lobster Pot social club. Marcus had built a large replica lobster pot for the bar. It had been a community project and everyone had pulled together to offer their skills for free to create a unique place for everyone to enjoy.

On the way back, Marcus wanted to get some milk from the supermarket. He stopped at ASDA, where my husband had always insisted on shopping. I was furious and refused to go inside, and I didn't want him to go in either. Slipping on my headphones, I listened to my mantras to calm down. I locked the car doors to feel more secure. Marcus took ages, which stressed me out. When he finally returned, he asked if I wanted some milk-bottle sweets—the same sweets he used to give us as kids. I was sulky at first but submitted to the sweets. As we sat in the car eating them, Marcus looked at the ASDA sign and said, "Andy Staines, Despicable Arsehole." It made me laugh. The milk-bottle sweets and the acronyms had dispelled my anger and I was happy again.

I was an emotional time bomb. My mind was like a sponge, picking up the slightest feeling and tuning into whatever was around me or my heightened emotions. For now, chewing those sweets whisked away my anxiety. Marcus admitted he was a bit on edge too, as while he was in ASDA, he "had a call from Dr Lovejoy about Stephanie's eyes." She was going in for an operation soon and the consultant called to discuss a few things. His name was hilarious and made us both laugh.

The next morning Marcus, Stephanie and I popped into their town centre to check out the debit card I had for our joint-bank account. I had opened it when we got married but Andy didn't want to use a joint account, so it was never used, or so I thought. In fact, he had been squirrelling away money and using it all along. I found the small sum of £400 and asked the woman at the counter if I could withdraw it. I explained that it was an account my husband and I didn't use, so I didn't expect there would be any money in there. She told me that four other customers had been in that morning and were splitting up with their partners too, and it was obviously the season for it.

We met Stephanie later and found ourselves in WHSmith. I wanted to buy a diary and one for next year as it was filled with positive and inspirational quotes. It said things like, Be Crazy. See the beauty in Everything. Love love love, leave a little sparkle wherever you go. It was brightly coloured and I felt I needed to look forward to 2015 when my life would hopefully be so different than it was at this time.

Every day in Dorset became an adventure itself, never knowing what was going to happen. That day, we were off to Poundbury together, someplace I'd never been. We had a walk around the place. Everything was so clean—too perfect, too quiet. It reminded me of the children's show I loved and watched as a kid, Trumpton or Camberwick Green, an animated cartoon. All the characters lived in a small town where people lived idyllic lives. They never spoke since they didn't have mouths. The narrator would ask questions, and they would wave or nod their heads. Prince Charles had been involved in the building and planning of this traditionalist model village as it was built on his Duchy Land Estate. I was told he had a house there and visited regularly. The architecture was based on the natural beauty of classical structures, and there were many grand buildings. This was probably another reason why it seemed so odd. We walked around and found a lovely café, which doubled up as an art gallery, and we had tea and lemon cake. There was an exhibition going on and I was absorbed by all the beautiful paintings. I found a triglyph of some amazing paintings that really spoke to me. They were three long rectangular landscapes. The first one was a solitary large white rock, abandoned but strong, that was exactly how I felt right then. Alone and isolated. The second one was of luminous green fields and representing pastures new. In my mind, I'd already decided I would move somewhere in the Dorset countryside and start afresh where no one knew me. The third one was of an ancient tree taking deep roots into the landscape. At the time I felt rootless, but somehow knew that in the future I would blossom into a new life.

Marcus and Stephanie were worried about my spending. I talked them through the paintings and how I felt they described my situation, alone and abandoned by my husband and the loss of my would-be children. The paintings gave me the hope and optimism I needed to carve out a future for myself. I had lost everything, including my mind. I was hypersensitive to everything and fragile mentally and physically. Since I had just found an unexpected £400 from my husband that would cover it. I bought the paintings, and was happy as I was building up my new life. The paintings were by the mother of the woman serving us in the shop. She worked under the name Hula Shine. The young shop assistant called her mother, who was delighted that I was buying all three, so she gave me a £50 discount. The images would serve as a reminder of what I had been through and where I was heading. There would be a life after all this, and it would just take some time to create it and get myself back together again.

Poundbury, in all its surreal perfection, felt like the movie set, The Truman Show. Marcus and Stephanie showed me the house Prince Charles owned and there was a garden behind it where he had created a personal tribute to Princess Diana, or so they said. His house was next door to a church and a small peaceful garden, a place of silent prayer. I never knew what was true or not, so much of my life had changed and everything seemed confusing.

While browsing the shop windows and architecture, I somehow lost Marcus and Stephanie. So I walked around on my own looking for Prince Charles's house. I thought maybe he could help me get my children back, so I knocked on the door of his house. A lady opened it and I told her my story. She looked at me blankly and said Prince Charles wasn't there and that I'd have to write to Clarence House. I felt embarrassed and left.

After visiting the memorial garden for Princess Diana, I suddenly felt a strong connection to her as though she had contacted me through her spirit. She told me after all that had happened to me, I wouldn't suffer financially. I would always be okay and she told me I won't have to worry about money again. I started to write down what she was saying to me. Perhaps, between my mental fragility and insomnia, my mind was picking up on the slightest of things and turning them into something.

I was working for a clairvoyant called Linda Jarrett who channelled information, so, in my fragile state it didn't seem that strange at all. Linda had channelled Princess Diana once before when I had a reading. She said at the time everything would be okay with me and the children, so I felt reassured and delighted at the time. Looking back, it's funny how your mind can play tricks on you when you are stressed beyond all limits and not sleeping.

That evening, despite my exhaustion, I couldn't sleep as usual. I never had problems sleeping before. I did a video call to my brother Tony in Australia, since he lived on the other side of the world it was in their waking hours of the day.

Throughout the night, I kept waking up, confused, wondering where my children were. In some ways, I felt Marcus and Stephanie were my surrogate children and sometimes they were my parents. They had slept in my children's beds, after all, and now they were caring for me in their home. I was staying in their spare room, they called it 'the junk room'. It felt appropriate in some weird way, since I, too, had been discarded. The room scared me a bit. In the dark, the paintings of Egyptian goddesses hanging on the walls seemed to come alive. I would glance at their piercing eyes watching me. On the bedside table, there was a photo of a child, about three years old, the same age as Isabella, wearing a pretty dress and strolling happily through a cemetery. I thought maybe the images were messages for me. In reality, these were just pictures Marcus and Stephanie had in their spare room of their children or from their trips abroad. In my clouded mind, those images would either provoke me or comfort me. The photo of the little girl, so sweet and carefree, was a reminder of what I had lost. Isabella hadn't died, but the plan to be her mother had been aborted. When my eyes fell on the life jacket in a dark corner, I thought the room was set up for me. The day before Marcus had jokingly said there was a life jacket there if I needed it. So it was funny but true, the life jacket was a metaphor of sorts.

On my first day at their house, I created an altar on the floor with all the small sacred objects that I had brought with me. I chanted all night long and felt like something spiritual was awakening within me. And I felt I was psychic at times. When I spoke to my brother in Australia, I told him that someone we knew had won the lottery. He showed me a bottle of champagne and said that an old school friend had. In this state, I had a habit of talking very fast or speaking like 'a sage' and repeating things three times. The symbol that kept coming back to me was that I was a grain of sand under a stone. I had nothing. I was worthy of nothing. On the other hand, I felt okay about this nothingness. I knew it, and I was safe as a grain of sand. A tiny dot.

It was a strange time for me and staying in an unfamiliar place with very old family friends added to the oddness. I was grateful to Marcus and Stephanie for opening their house and giving their time to care for me. I felt like a small, helpless child, but I had to just do the work. That was, make the calls, and do all the stuff to readjust to my new life. To cope with everything, I had to become an actress, too, pretending I was normal and standing up for myself. Every day there was some kind of work for me to do. I thought Marcus was using some psychological tests to help me get through this mess. He had a set of ideas, he would say for me to "park something" when there were worries or things we couldn't sort out, and I could then revisit them later. A term I had never heard before, but when I got overwhelmed it seemed to work.

Sometimes people told me things that I couldn't discern if they were telling the truth or not. Stephanie told me about the 'ferret man' who lived across the road and he had asked her if she wanted to go ferreting. I was freaked out by this story and avoided looking at the houses opposite. The ferret man reminded me of the flasher I had while living alone in London. Whenever I went past this particular apartment building, he would tap on his window loudly to draw my attention. When I looked up, he'd flash me. I felt disgusted and threatened by him. I guess it was bringing up a time in my life when I was living alone in a new area of London and felt vulnerable. During these nights, I had flashbacks of the bad things that had happened to me. It was like my soul was creating a reckoning of incidents and moments, and either resolving those conflicts or reminding me to let them go. Creepy men from my past crept up on me. Abuse popped up, not that I had been abused. Or perhaps I had. Surely the actions of my husband were abusive. I had unwittingly allowed him to slip a knife into my heart that had gone in too deep and had been stuck there ever since. I had to now live with it in my heart.

Stephanie was going to have her operation soon with Dr Lovejoy, so she and Marcus tried to prepare me for going back home and emptying the house of the children's things. They planned to take me home the very next day. Marcus and Stephanie had a lot of empathy for my situation, but nothing could have prepared me for what was to follow.

8

Week Three: The Long Drive Home

The sunshine of a new day was peeking through the curtains. I was going back to the place that was once my home. I had mixed feelings, but I was now open to whatever came along each day. I didn't have much sense of time. Marcus and Stephanie were going to help me to pack up all the things I had gathered for the children. Marcus had told me, and trained me, along the way to empower myself. Somehow, with their constant encouragement through all of this, I mustered up the courage and energy to keep going.

Marcus knew I couldn't have the children on my own, but he needed me to admit that to myself by taking action. I knew this, but my will to have them was so strong, I kept on deluding myself. For starters, he felt the best thing to do was to empty the house of the children's toys and things before I could live there again.

After a long drive, we got back to mine. I hadn't been there for over a week. Laura and Sara were already there. Sara was upset and kept asking me about her husband's website, some problem with the email, and if I could fix it.

"Sara," I snapped, "I can't cope with anything, let alone fixing someone's website."

Her lips quivered and her big brown eyes welled with tears. I found it hard to look at her. Turning away, I had work to do and I was here to empty my house of all the things I had bought for the children. In retrospect, my sister was showing me the feelings that I was unable to express. She felt heartbroken for me.

I wandered around the house, room by room, emptying whatever I could find. Toys were laid out ready for the children to explore. A beautiful wooden rocking chair, big enough for the two of them. I was taking the objects through the house into the garage and Sara and Laura were filling their cars. I went into what would have been Isabella's room. My niece had given me her fairy quilt set and I had bought a Peppa Pig toy, as it was a favourite of hers.

I didn't cry, I just did the work as Marcus had trained me to do. It was all done quickly, running up and down the stairs, moving objects out of the house and into their waiting cars. Although I felt disturbed by Sara's emotions. Why was she being so emotional? These were my children I had lost.

My life was becoming a performance, some kind of tragic play, and the show had to go on. The place was like a conveyer belt of people moving objects from house to car, creating and making some kind of order. Once the house was emptied, Marcus thought it was a good idea for me to call Helen's husband Frank and see how things were progressing on his side.

I rang Frank and the first thing I asked is, "So are you and Helen getting a divorce ?"

"I've seen a solicitor," he said quietly and skilfully changing the subject, "You know you could get some of Andy's pension."

"But you've known for weeks that your wife's having an affair with my husband and done nothing. What are you going to do about it?" I yelled down the phone, which was out of character for me.

"You seem to be pretending like everything's fine. It's NOT FINE."

Marcus wanted me to get angry with Frank so the reality would sink in that I had lost my children, my husband, and my life as I knew it. I think he was angry about how Andy and Helen's callousness had upended my world. I didn't know what I was doing, but now that I had lost my children, I didn't want Frank to lose his. Not realising that he wouldn't—it was just me losing my dreams.

I was confused, depleted and my brain wasn't working properly.

We were on the phone for about a good hour. Looking back, I wished Frank had just told me to piss off and hung up on me, since I was acting like a nutter. Sure, I was going through a nightmare and losing my grip on reality. I just couldn't believe my husband, the man who I had loved and thought loved me could do this in such a damaging way.

Marcus had been encouraging me to let off steam with Frank since he'd known for five or six weeks. He thought it would empower me to express my emotions. This dip into anger mode had left me, but it could flare up again at any moment.

To be fair, Frank had confronted Andy and warned him to stay away from his wife. As soon as they returned from Uganda, he'd also sent Andy some beers and a card saying sarcastically, thanks for looking after my wife in Africa, knowing full well they were having an affair. Andy hadn't got the hint though. It had been too little, too late by then. The relationship had already happened, and they worked together so they were hardly able to stay away from each other. They had hatched their plan.

Much later, when I went to visit Frank, he confided that he had been monitoring his wife's phone messages and social media. While my husband had casually admitted to me that Helen slept in our house when I was over at my sister's the weekend before the adoption. She had probably slept in our bed. He said they didn't, but he had turned out to be a liar and a bad one. I was the one losing out, stupidly in the dark. His sheer callousness was abusive. I mean, Helen had had dinner at our table, in our dining room surrounded by our future children's toys. Did either of them have a conscience? All I knew was in that moment I had lost everything, and was on my way to losing my sanity.

Given that I had just emptied my whole house of all the children's things, and stripped it bare within an hour, I guess it was the only way to cope. A deeply emotional experience on a subconscious level, but I couldn't allow my feelings to come up. Sara, however, was distraught. I felt all my emotions just looking at her face, which it made it harder for me to cope. I had to stay strong and show everyone I was able to cope with this bizarre situation. It was all done like an undercover operation. We were erasing my past, and all the love and effort I had put into creating a home for those two sweet little kids.

Marcus and Stephanie didn't think it was a good idea for me to stay at my house. They were all wary of Andy turning up and what he might do. Instead, I would leave my car in the drive making out I was still living there. It was decided for me that I would stay at my older sister's house for the time being. It seemed like the only option, so I grabbed a few things and went off with Laura. She had a spare room and Mum lived in a granny's annexe next door. I would be safe there out of the dangerous clutches of my erratic and unstable husband.

In hindsight, staying at the house would have been more sensible. I could've come to terms with it within my familiar environment, not going to yet another unfamiliar room, in another bed. Adapting to all these different places was destabilising.

In times of crisis like this, families stick together. Over the years I had helped Laura, especially when her children were very young and Dad was dying, so she could spend more time with him. I felt supported by my big brother Tom who had come down on the day and dropped everything and lent me money since I no longer had access to the joint-bank account.

I had moved to a small village in Hampshire, thankfully Laura lived on the edge of the village. My husband worked in the village school, where he continued to teach, and life just went on for him. Andy was teaching Helen's son. They had arranged this together at the school. She got what she wanted and now she had him too. Realistically, even if he wanted to stay, I had no use for him after what he had done. It would only be a matter of time before he would do something to her.

The shock of that terrible morning of him kneeling by the bedside while I was half-asleep kept flooding back to me. Those words "I don't want the children and I have feelings for Helen" would be forever seared in my brain. I would have a whole lifetime to live without those gorgeous little children and wouldn't ever be a mother. Very few people will understand how this feels and still feels deep in my heart as time goes on.

A new place to stay and I was lucky I have family who cared about me. I moved into my sister's spare room. Laura had a lovely farmhouse, painted in pale, beachy colours, with a huge garden filled with fruit trees and beautiful flowers. They had hens and, of course, Monty, their gentle yellow Lab.

I got settled into my room. I had torches galore, just in case. Often, I'd wake up around 4 am and get up. It didn't make sense to stay in bed if I couldn't sleep. I was scared every night I went to sleep, despairing about the unpredictability of everything. I kept it together by day, but the nights were long and unbearable.

On a brighter note, on my return from Dorset, I had gifts for everyone. It was as if I had been on holiday and bought them all gifts, like I did as a kid. I gathered them in my Mum's lounge room and told them all about meeting Chris the sage, and showed them the stone I'd bought and how it had predicted my "short duration personal saviour". I showed them my paintings and explained how I would emerge from the ashes of the great big bonfire that had become my life. I gave them all the scarves and a bar of rose or lemon soap for the girls and Indian sandalwood soap for the guys. They all looked happy, or so I thought. It was as if I had been on a normal holiday.

Patrick, Laura's husband, seemed to love his yellow scarf and said it was his favourite colour. I felt like I was like a Buddha or holy person and had grown spiritually on my trip to Dorset, now being more connected to the higher worlds. My senses were heightened into a different realm and I was optimistic about my future.

The next day I decided I wanted to shed my past. I was letting go of my marriage and ripping up the small paintings I had made and throwing them out the window. Ed, my nephew, was running around outside with Monty and collecting all the little pieces for me. I didn't know what to do with myself, with these sudden surges of emotion that I needed to release. It was unnerving to be so close to where my husband was happily at work, pretending life was normal. Nearby Helen and her children were also happily getting on with their lives while I was suspended into this crushing new reality of uncertainty and nothingness.

I had no one to talk to since everyone around me was just as distressed by my situation. They didn't know what to do with me. I'm sure I was becoming unpredictable and tiring. I had a sense of euphoria and convinced myself that I would cope with the sudden end of my marriage and the loss of adoptive children. I wanted to make everything better for everyone. I saw how it affected my family and didn't want my friends to suffer, so I didn't tell any of them or contact them for support. I just stayed in my family bubble. If I was being clear-eyed and rational, I would've realised that this only isolated me further.

I wasn't sleeping at night during the first week. I felt my heart was just going to stop, break in half, like two teacups clashing together, over and over again. I've never been afraid of death. How does anyone cope with the pain of such a sudden loss? Still, I put on a brave face and positive attitude during the day. When I recall all the profiles of the children we saw, those little faces and then read about their sad lives, I felt upset. What had they done wrong? Just to be born into a family that was unable to provide a stable life for them. Often the parents' lives had been of suffering and neglect, and so their children followed the path of being neglected too. My heart bled for them. All they wanted was to be loved and cared for, and all I wanted was to love and care for them. Clearly, the universe had decided that my life would take a different path. Instead of getting used to the idea, I was suspended in a kind of shock.

I only stayed at Laura's for two nights. One night when I couldn't sleep, I went downstairs and had a lie down on my Mum's sofa. She was awake and put the TV on. I couldn't bear to look at it. She seemed pissed off with me, probably because she was tired and worried about my odd and irrational behaviour. I was scared of the images on the TV and thought that the adoption agency was monitoring me via the TV. They were testing me to see if I could cope with this situation and if I could I still adopt the children on my own.

Seeing my restlessness, my mother told me to open my mouth and popped in a small sleeping pill. When I woke up the next day, I was distressed and dazed from the Valium. The effects hadn't worn off. I kept remembering all the documents I had read about the abuse of the children in care—now I felt that I had been abused. I couldn't trust my husband. Now I could no longer trust my family either. My past experiences started flooding back to me. I was losing control and falling fast down a big black hole of exhaustion and confusion.

9

A Parallel Universe

Sitting slumped at the kitchen in a Valium haze, I stared out the window in hunched- shouldered silence. Laura agreed to drive me to a meditation morning with Linda Jarrett in West Sussex. She thought it might help me relax with my insomnia. My sister lived near the A3 motorway and I swear I heard moving traffic whooshing by all night long. It made my already-rattled mind feel busy. I had been to many of Linda's healing and meditation workshops over the past few years. She had also commissioned me to do some regular graphic design work for her.

Since I no longer had access to my car, Laura took me there and I was nattering all the way. I had so much going on that I needed to express. I put my headphones on to try and stop the interference going on in my head. My sister was laughing at me. By this point, after two torturous weeks of sleeplessness, my body and mind were worn-out and drained.

When we got to the meditation centre, I was exhausted and on high alert. Linda whisked me inside. Laura decided she wouldn't stay but went off to get coffee somewhere alone and have a break—probably from me.

The meditation space, held in a local community centre, was a familiar place and I found a seat in the circle. The meditations were powerful as I lay on the floor, I could feel the weight of everything being released from me. I felt safe here, but a little on edge too. Not sure what might come out of my mouth, I decided not to say very much. I kept channelling a monk, who was giving me messages that made so much sense. I felt a deep connection to universal oneness. The meditation was calming. It attuned me into slowing down my mind and body, leaving me feeling restored.

So it had worked, I thought. I was acting normal again, sort of. During the healing session, the woman who was working on me, came out with some powerful messages for me. I told her she would receive a gift. It felt like I was getting help from my spiritguides to get me through this terrible time and there would be a gift for me when I reached my new life.

On the way back, I offered to take my sister out for lunch as a thank-you for taking me to the meditation group. There was a quirky beachfront café in the shape of a huge beach pebble in Littlehampton. Since it was packed, I suggested taking a walk along the beach and coming back later. Along the shore, I saw a little boy with blonde hair, the same age as Alfie, on a little push bike, who turned around and looked me straight in the eye. He couldn't take his eyes off me and gave me a beautiful smile. He seemed to say to me telepathically, "I will see you soon" and waved as he rode off.

I began seeing people as lookalikes everywhere. Guess this happens when you are beyond exhausted. I knew this, as years ago this happened on tour when I was in the Auteurs, a semi-successful indie band in the vein of other 90s indie rock/pop groups like Suede, Pulp and Radiohead. My boyfriend Luke was the songwriter/lead guitarist of the band and we went on tour to Japan. With a gig practically every day, in Tokyo, Nagoya, Osaka and other cities, I hadn't slept for a week and along with the Blade Runner-like sensory overload of skyscrapers and buzzing neon lights, my mind went into overdrive.

When Laura and I wandered back to the beach café, there was a table free for us. A friend came rushing out of the café, "Hi Alice, how are you?" She assumed that I was on my lockdown week with the children. I lied and said that I was good, trying to sound convincing. In truth at that moment, I did feel okay and had momentarily forgotten about the mess of my life. I couldn't let her know, not now, out in public that I didn't have the children. I would've probably crumbled right there on the spot. In British culture, many of us don't honestly say how we are when someone asks. I had been meticulously trained to keep calm and carry on even if the house was on fire. It would've been too devastating, to tell the truth when I was still in such shock myself. Either that or I was still in deep denial I would live a life of childlessness. Whatever the reason, I couldn't deal with other people's emotions when I could barely deal with my own.

Settling in a corner table, I glanced around the café at the huge windows and out to the glimmer of sea beyond. It felt good to enjoy the relaxing atmosphere with my sister. We laughed about ordering the same food and had a good chat. It was like old times before I got married. Afterwards, we drove to a place called Bosham, a cute little coastal hamlet near Chichester, and had afternoon tea in a quaint coffee shop overlooking the water. Again, we had a lovely time catching up, it was like old times going on day trips. The café had been empty when we first arrived and we watched it slowly filling up. I noticed some people looked normal and others seemed strangely reptilian. I could feel the difference in people's energy very clearly. I told Laura and she said she felt it too. It was if I could almost see a little beyond the 3D world and things that were normally invisible to the human eye. After a while, seeing this quick glimpse of a reptilian man sitting near us, we both felt this and had to leave.

Strolling around the harbour, Laura and I talked openly about why we hadn't been so close, these last seven years. As a big family, we had all gone our own ways in life. I had moved nearer to Laura but this closeness in proximity hadn't helped our relationship.

I turned to her warily, staring at the patch of blue sky behind her, and asked. "You always seem uneasy around me. What have I done?"

"I didn't like your husband," she replied honestly.

"Wow... so for seven years you didn't like him, so you couldn't be my sister. And after seven days, I'd decided he wasn't going to be a part of my life and I'd never speak to him again."

We both laughed and continued our walk along the shore.

"He treated me so badly. And it makes me sad that you suffered and lost out on our friendship because of him."

What a funny world we live in. I had to lose my marriage and children to be friends with my sister again. I had spent the last seven years thinking it was me she disliked, not him.

On the drive back, Marcus called and we chatted briefly until I noticed the call had a 555 number and I thought my phone was being tapped. Suddenly paranoid that we were being followed, I threw my phone out the window into a nearby bush. I later realised it was anxiety about what Andy was going to do about getting back into the house. I made Laura stop the car and insisted she get rid of her phone and the kindle she had with her. I said to put them in a plastic bag which she did and leave them in a ditch, so she could get them back later. Seeing my distress, she didn't argue. I persuaded her to drive me to Chithurst Buddhist Monastery, thinking I'd be safe there. Housed in an old coach house in a 150-acre forest in Sussex, it was an overseas branch of a lineage of 'forest monasteries' in northern Thailand.

When we got there, I slunk off into the meditation room and lit some incense. It was peaceful. I rang the bell and a monk and a female layperson came inside and sat with me. I told them my story and they didn't say anything. I said I didn't trust the woman, I didn't like her energy. She didn't seem to like me either. So she left and was replaced by a young Dutch monk.

So I sat with the young monk and the old sterner monk and rambled on. The young Dutch monk seemed to understand me. The older higher-up monk, his face curved into a frown, seemed angry. I begged them to listen, but the older monk said they didn't have long and had things to do. We all moved outside and sat in an alcove of a pretty tranquil garden.

Desperate for help, I asked them for their advice.

The surly old monk asked me the same question back. "Well, how will you manage this situation? How are you going to live the rest of your life?"

"I don't know. I guess I'll just have to take one day at a time," I said and, after a thought, added, "I'm half Buddhist." He nodded sullenly.

I honestly thought they would be able to help me. I wanted safe passage back to Dorset since I didn't feel safe in Hampshire, being so close to my ex. I was paranoid that people were out to get me, since any security I had in my life had gone. The older monk took me back inside and wouldn't let me speak. He'd obviously had enough of me. He sat me in another room. Since he wouldn't allow me to talk, I started using magazines and books, creating words to communicate my plight. I managed to make up a sentence for them to read: Help me, listen to me.

They both looked at it. The younger monk laughed at my weird behaviour. I felt he understood me better and had some compassion for my situation. Feeling grateful, I tried to give him my camera and my watch. He wouldn't accept them. My sister, unnerved by the whole episode, was with the older monk. She was frantically trying to call her husband, but only had numbers that she could remember off by heart since I had made her leave her phone in the ditch. It was all my fault and Laura was cross with me. I was stretching her to the limit, but all I wanted was to feel safe somewhere. The last place I could recall feeling safe was in the junk room at Marcus and Stephanie's house in Dorset.

The monks had been my last resort. I thought that the Buddhists would have some useful answers, particularly since my family were fed up. I needed emotional support and someone to listen to me. But who? When I went back into the room where my sister and the older monk were, they gave me a stern look and I returned to the other room. Eventually, Laura's husband Patrick came and took us home to their house. We didn't discuss what happened. I quietly went to my room and felt bad about upsetting Laura and the mess I had made of the day.

Over breakfast the next morning, not knowing what else to do with me, Patrick and Laura suggested taking me to the hospital. I hated hospitals. All the sadness and sterility sapped my energy and optimism.

"I think you need to see a doctor," Laura said. She knew I needed professional help and was doing this with my best interest at heart. "Alice, you can't continue like this."

"Like what?" She was saying she'd had enough of me. In my sleep-deprived haze, I started thinking maybe I should call Sara or someone to get me out of here. After a while, I said, "I know I'm messy, flawed, confused. But I'm not insane."

Laura pressed on, "I never said you were... just that it would help you."

I wasn't sure exactly how it would help me but agreed since I felt cornered. At the time it was clear to me my grief, sadness and crumbling life was a source of shame and too much for her.

Moments later, the three of us were sitting in the waiting room. I moved seats a few times, not wanting to sit beside Laura or Patrick. I knew they were just trying to get rid of me. They thought I would run away, and I felt threatened and trapped. Without a phone, I couldn't even call a friend for help.

After a long, interminable wait and not speaking to each other, the doctor finally came out. She seemed like a nice lady, asked me some questions, she said she couldn't do anything for me as I wasn't a danger to others or myself and so she prescribed some mild anti-depressants and sent us on our way. Then the three of us left together. Laura and Patrick looked mystified that the doctor wasn't going to do anything to help me. I had clearly become a huge liability to them.

When we got back in the car, we went to the beach. I wanted to see Dad or rather be near where his ashes were scattered. I wanted to feel close to someone who I knew loved me. During the first few days after that nightmarish morning, before going to Dorset, Mum, Laura, Sara and I spent some time in a lovely café on the beach, trying to come to terms with what had happened. Now the café was closed and it had started to rain.

I was happy walking in the rain along the beach. I didn't care about getting wet and felt alive in the rain. Laura and Patrick were worried and wanted to take me back to the car.

"It's only a little rain and it's lovely," I said, enjoying the sensation of the trickling rain and the feeling of freedom. As the downpour intensified, so did the general mood. Laura and Patrick looked uneasy and exasperated. Once I was back in the car, soaked to the bone, I didn't like this feeling at all. Laura immediately took off her jeans and gave them to me. That was thoughtful and kind of her.

We ended up driving around Old Portsmouth, a pretty medieval town with cobbled streets, quaint pubs and historic tearooms. I felt trapped in the car since the child locks were on and I couldn't get out. I found my sister's counselling boxes in the back of the car. Boxes in bright colours and different sizes that all make up one box, kind of like those Russian nesting dolls. I was placing them inside one another to prove to them I was still normal, but they weren't convinced. I was scared and, at that moment, my greatest fear was getting locked up.

Laura left the car for what felt like a long time and dropped by a friend's house "to make some calls". Being eight years older than me and conscientious, Laura cast herself in the role as my care-giver. It was suffocating. All I wanted to do was to get to Dorset and see Marcus and Stephanie. They were nice to me down there. At Laura's house, I only felt trapped and anxious. It was dark by the time Laura returned to the car. I was struck by her glumness and unease. Guess she hadn't had any luck with whatever plans she had to get rid of me. She obviously didn't want me to go back to her house for fear of what I would do next. And I didn't want to be there either.

Unsure of how to deal with me and frankly fed up, Laura slumped in the front seat in quiet defeat.

Seeing her despair, I said, "Can you take me to Kelly's house?"

Kelly was my oldest friend and would look after me. Since I didn't have my phone, I couldn't call her and just had to turn up on her doorstep on a Sunday night. Thankfully she was in and the house was full of smoke when we all walked in. Kelly and her husband John were chilling out, smoking and drinking wine.

After Laura and Patrick left hurriedly, Kelly and I, moved into the kitchen to have a proper catch up, leaving John in the living room watching television. We sat down at the kitchen table and Kelly opened another bottle of wine.

"Your sister didn't look very happy," she said, as she refilled my glass. "Is everything alright?"

"Everything's terrible," I replied, holding back the tears. "Andy and I are divorcing." "What?! What about the kids?"

"He's run off with Helen a teacher, at his school and the adoption isn't happening."

"God, that's awful," she said quietly. "What a terrible bastard."

"I'm not bothered about him, but the children." I went quiet, and the sadness of what I just said hit me. I wiped my eyes. "I would've given them a great life. I haven't met them, but I loved them."

In shock, she got up and hugged me. We drank some more wine. I felt the freedom of being away from the entrapment of my sister. My mind was sensitive, and we continued to drink late into the evening. At one point, I told Kelly my body must be shrinking as my jeans felt baggy and massive. I'd forgotten I was wearing my sister's jeans.

It was just me and Kelly in her kitchen like in the good old days, drinking and momentarily the stress of my current life seemed to disappear. A little tipsy, I said to Kelly, "Imagine if our favourite boyfriend came knocking on the door. Who would yours be?"

She laughed and said, "Probably Brad Pitt."

"I meant guys that we know. Mine would've been Damon." He was a guy I had a huge crush on for many years when we were at school. He liked me too, but we never got together, mainly because I was too shy. At that moment, feeling quite pissed, I imagined he'd magically turned up at Kelly's house. I went to look for him at the front door but there was no one there. We eventually finished up and I crashed on her sofa and, for the first time in a week, actually nodded off, exhausted by the alcohol and the sheer challenge of the day

10

The Fateful Day

I was living in a lonely place of no trust. I felt like a fugitive, on the run from my old life. There was no turning back. Woken up by the faint wintry light streaming into Kelly's living room, I got up. I'd fallen asleep in my clothes and felt like I was swimming in my jeans. I thought my body must have been inexplicably shrinking overnight. I'd forgotten that I borrowed another pair of jeans from Kelly the night before. They were still too loose and I had to hold them up as I walked along the street. I decided to walk into Southsea to get a pair of new jeans. Walking along the road in clothes that didn't fit me made me feel vulnerable.

Sensing that someone was following me, I turned around and saw Kelly's husband John behind me. Why on earth was he following me? Or was he just walking into town too?

When I tried to cross the road, he stood in front of me, blocking my path. I felt intimidated, but he didn't seem to care. He later told Kelly that I had tried to get run over walking into the road. This was ridiculous, but everyone believed him and not me. I was only trying to avoid him. All I wanted to do was to go into Southsea and buy a pair of Levi's that fit me.

Within ten minutes an ambulance and police car had been called. Before I realised what was happening, Kelly was in the street in her pyjamas and I was trying to talk my way out of this—whatever this was. I hadn't done anything wrong. Surely, I wasn't that badly off that they had to call the police.

Reluctantly, I agreed to get into the police car and they drove us back to Kelly's house. The policewoman, Rebecca, whom I started calling Ra, was muscular and fit, she looked like a strong woman. I asked her who her hero was. She told me it was Juliet Bravo, the police detective in the series of the same name. I told her my story and, miraculously, she listened. She had a younger male officer with her, and I asked him, "What's your ideal job?" He said he wanted to be a fireman, so I gave him a nickname too, Sam, after Fireman Sam. I was trying to be light-hearted and chatty, so they would realise I wasn't mad or a danger to anyone.

I thought I had to use delay tactics and chattered compulsively, so they wouldn't lock me up. John had rung Laura and Patrick, who were on their way down to get me. Behind my back, Laura and Patrick had called Crisis at Home, a crisis-intervention service, like I was some kind of nutter, and they were on their way too.

This isn't right, I remember thinking, Why had they called the emergency services for a woman walking down the street? I'd never been in trouble with the police but was starting to feel like a hostage in the back of their patrol car. The only thing they hadn't done was handcuff me. But they wouldn't let me go until my sister and the Crisis at Home people had arrived. Anxious and hungover from the day before, I started rattling on about spiritual things and asking them about numbers. Out of nowhere, I became obsessed with numbers and their meanings, unaware of how odd I sounded. I guess they could say I was acting like I was mentally unstable, since I was talking so fast and from one wild tangent to another. By this point, as sad as it sounded, I trusted the police more than I did my friends Kelly and John.

Eventually, a tall, slender white woman in her late-50s arrived. She was accompanied by a quiet and sweet-looking young black man in his mid-to-late 20s. They were from Crisis at Home and had come to assess my mental state. They persuaded me to sit in Kelly's lounge, I sat upright in the middle of her big green sofa. They sat adjacent to me, squeezed together on the smaller sofa.

The woman explained why they were here and asked, "Would you like anyone, a family member or friend, to join us?"

"No, I'd prefer to be alone."

"My colleague here is a trainee," she said, looking over at the young black man.

The pair of them sat huddled together, observing me for any signs of abnormality. As they stared at me intensely, I could feel my hands tensing up. They started firing off questions. I knew what they said was important, but I didn't trust them. My brain was going like the clappers. I tried to focus on the questions they asked and answered honestly. I had come to Kelly's house for help, hoping as a good friend, that she would be able to see beyond my symptoms and give me a safe place to crash for a little while, but instead plunged me into a deeper sense of entrapment.

After they had finished peppering me with questions, the woman asked, "Would you like us to share the details with anyone?"

I shrugged. "No." Laura and her husband had just arrived, but I definitely didn't trust them and had nothing to say to them.

The Crisis at Home woman suggested getting some mild anti-depressants and in the future she said some mindfulness would be useful. Surprisingly she respected my need for privacy and left without talking to my sister or friend. I felt relieved she wasn't going to lock me up. She was used to assessing people, so she could probably see I wasn't mad, but just sad and anxious.

Later, in a moment of clarity, I realised it was a mistake not to allow the Crisis at Home woman to share the information. Maybe they would have accepted her assessment and allowed me to rest up and get better. Instead, my sister and my friends were now panicking. They wanted to control me and put me in a place where they control unmanageable people like me. Thanks to my oldest sister Laura and oldest friend Kelly, I was getting stressed out and creating a bigger hole for myself.

After that unnecessary drama subsided and the crisis people left, I thought to myself, I don't trust any of you, and spun out of the house to head into town. But now, annoyingly, I was in hot pursuit by Laura, Kelly and both their husbands. To shake them off, I dived into a Chinese restaurant owned by a friend of my brother's and sat down. I started chatting with the guy and told him I was trying to contact Tom, but I had lost my phone and no longer had his number.

Laura rushed in and saw me there but wouldn't speak to me. She looked pissed off and walked back out again. I sat and felt protected by this man, since he was my brother's mate, even though I hardly knew him. He had gone to the same secondary school as Tom. Not wanting to alarm him, I didn't bother telling him my story. I just sat there and he fed me some fresh vegetable spring rolls and casually mentioned that the shop would be closing soon. I wondered how I was going to escape from the people that were hunting me now. Again, I started to think that maybe I was being tested by the adoption agency so I can still have the children.

I looked outside the restaurant door, which appeared safe, and slowly made my way back into Southsea. I popped into a phone shop to buy a cheap phone. I sat down and waited, but since the service was slow, I wandered into John Lewis and found some clothes to wear. I picked up a navy coat and a blue dress with a little pattern on it. Alone in the changing room, while I trying the dress on, Laura and Kelly suddenly appeared outside the curtain. Ignoring them, I told the assistant I wanted to wear all the clothes from the shop. As I was paying, Kelly asked for the jeans she lent me that morning and angrily snatched them from me. She was the one person I thought I could trust. She was siding with my hysterical sister and, instead of showing me some empathy and kindness, she betrayed me.

All I could think of was how I could get away from them. So I kept running and disappeared into a nearby café. Predictably, Patrick, Laura's husband, had turned up and stood outside menacingly and wouldn't let me pass. I felt threatened, stalked, abused—and hated the lot of them. Out of desperation, I turned to the woman working in the café, but she didn't want to know. Outside, Laura had slipped in the rain and was slumped on the pavement crying angry tears. I felt bad since it was my fault that she'd fallen.

Reluctantly, I submitted to their wishes and I did what I was told and I got in the car with them. Neither Laura, Patrick nor Kelly were talking to me now. They were acting as if I was invisible. As we crawled along in a huge traffic jam on our way to Portchester, I turned to Kelly, who was sitting in the backseat beside me.

"Kelly, can you please help?" I asked in a half-whisper. "I don't want to see the doctor."

"You've done it now," she replied coldly. They were all at their wits and seemed to be ganging up on me.

"What've I done wrong? I am asking as a friend, please can you help me."

She just looked away, transfixed by her phone.

"What are you looking at?"

She flashed her phone, showing me photos of baby platypuses, fuzzy, flat-headed, duck-billed marine mammals that looked a bit like a cross between a seal and a duck. Though I love animals and nature, inexplicably, those pictures freaked me out. I thought she was acting weird while I was in this crisis.

What the fuck have I done wrong to these people?

The jarringly quiet atmosphere in the car was excruciating. When we slowed to a stop in heavy traffic, I tried to run out, but couldn't since they had the child-safety locks on. Everyone was now ignoring me in the car.

They appeared to be more concerned about being late to see the psychiatrist than me. Pulling up outside a shabby-looking building, behind a shabby-looking shopping centre, in Fareham, Laura and Kelly escorted me to the door of the clinic. Unsure of how to deal with this and frankly exhausted by Laura and the lot of them, I went inside willingly. They didn't want to come in and support me, which was fine since I no longer trusted any of them. Still, I couldn't help feeling hurt and abandoned by my oldest friend and my sister.

Inside the clinic waiting room, I noticed a distressed woman sitting on her own in a sad, crumpled heap. She looked like a drug addict in her dirty, raggedy clothes. I felt sorry for her and realised her 'crime' was that she was probably homeless. In a far corner, I saw another skinny middle-aged woman, with mascara-streaked tears streaming down her face, in a bad state. I wandered over and asked if she was okay. Then a nurse came out and led me into an office. I took one look at the psychiatrist, a grey-haired man with a cold face and even colder blue eyes, and felt petrified. I suspected Laura and Patrick told him that I was crazy. As he unleashed a flood of questions, I had a terrible feeling that he would lock me up. I scanned around the room for an escape route. There was a door wide open, I ran out and found myself in the car park outside.

By the time I left his office and got out of the building, it was quite dark outside. I wandered into the car park and, spotting a policeman, I asked him if he was really was one. I just didn't know who to trust now. Intimidatingly, he just stood staring at me blankly and he didn't say anything. I noticed the camera on his lapel filming me.

Behind him, I turned to see another policeman and the psychiatrist talking to Laura and Patrick, and Kelly pointing at me across the lot. This was maddening—a huge overreaction. Why couldn't they leave me alone? I felt wounded, bereft, and betrayed. Eventually, I couldn't take it any more and I screamed at the top of my lungs. I felt like a caged animal, collapsing on the ground, screaming. It was my last cry for help.

I had been mistreated, chased and held against my will. All the stories I read about abused children during the adoption process coursed through my mind in terrible, painful detail. When I saw the flashing lights of an ambulance heading toward me, I remembered hearing about the abuse of my music teacher from secondary school who was later imprisoned for abusing girls at my school.

Lying in a crumpled ball in tears, I surrendered to the medics. They scooped me off the ground into the ambulance and strapped me down. The nurse, who sat beside me, had a soft voice and angelic appearance and helped calm me down. She had a sweet, tender face and I could see she was kind. I told her I had been abused, which wasn't far from the truth since I'd been mentally abused by my husband.

A policeman accompanied us in the ambulance and I asked him to hold my thumb until I got to the hospital. He clasped my thumb for the whole journey and I felt grateful for his compassion.

Little did I know the worst was yet to come.

11

Strange New World

Waking up in a blindingly-bright white room, I found myself alone in a strange bed. In front of me was a set of barred windows facing a brick wall. The single door leading out of this room was thick and heavy, and I knew that it was locked from the outside. I instantly felt confused and claustrophobic. Yet, at the same time, the vast emptiness of the space overwhelmed me. My first thought was that I was in prison or some kind of detention centre. Panicked, I tried to remember how I got here. Or if I had paid for the clothes at John Lewis. Was I in here for shoplifting? If I had committed a crime, no one had told me about it yet. Perhaps I had been abducted and taken somewhere for torture. Maybe Andy paid someone to kidnap me, so he could take the house. Am I a bad wife? I must be. But I know I am not a bad person. If only someone would come in and give me a chance to explain myself. I'm certain that I am no danger to anyone, including myself. Was I brought here to be tortured or experimented on?

Glancing around, I saw someone peering through the window. It was creepy, like being watched by a peeping tom. What could he possibly find interesting watching me sitting in the bed? When the man disappeared from view, I crept up to the tiny, slatted window and peeked out. The man, who looked to be in his 50s with dark hair, a short-back-and-sides cut, was talking to a young woman. In the glow of the hallway light, the woman, whose soft face was quivering, appeared to be crying. Maybe they were in a relationship and he was treating her poorly. Why else would she be crying?

The man, seeing me, quickly closed the slats. I waved and knocked on the window, but they both pretended not to see me.

What is this place? When will I get out of here?

I climbed back into the strange bed, which, distressingly made me think of what happened a few weeks ago in my own bed. The shock of my husband's revelation. I wondered where in the world could I feel safe. I pulled my head under my sheets. My heart was pounding, but I knew I needed to stay calm.

Surely, once I could explain that I wasn't supposed to be here, they would let me go. But go where? I had no home to go back to.

I needed to go to the bathroom, but realised there wasn't one in this room. Scanning around, I noticed a button on the wall beside the bed and pressed it. I could only hear static at the other end. I didn't speak, suddenly afraid of who might come in. I kept pressing the button repeatedly until someone came in and took me to the toilet. The same man who'd been waiting for me outside the door guided me back into that room. The door closed and locked behind me once again.

Was I going to remain here forever?

The only thing I knew was Laura, Kelly and their husbands were angry with me and probably had me locked up.

The door swung open and a tall, youngish, sandy-haired guy I hadn't seen before walked in and looked at me warily. Scared of what he might do, I tried to get up but he told me to stay in the bed. He had bought me some drinks—they were probably spiked. Nothing about this feels right. Placing the three plastic cups on the windowsill, he left the room. I tiptoed across the room and peered into the cups. One had coffee, one tea and the other water. I drank all three in the same order he had placed them—coffee, tea and then water. Maybe since I have done what I was told, they would let me out. Then, dashing back to the bed, I buried my head beneath the covers, hoping this was only a bad dream and it would fade away soon.

An eternity seemed to pass. How much time, I have no idea. There were no clocks. But they seemed to have rules. I had to figure out what I was supposed to do next. I kept looking through the gaps in the blinds, but everyone kept acting as though I was invisible.

Perhaps this was some sort of a fucked-up social experiment. They were waiting for me to go mad, and then they would leave me to die. Doesn't that happen to people who no longer fit into society? Like in Victorian times when so-called hysterical women were shut away. If they weren't crazy to begin with, they certainly were once institutionalised. I thought of a book I'd read, The Yellow Wallpaper, about a woman who was left to lie, day after day, in an attic room until she went mad, escaping into the wallpaper. But I know I am not mad. Just sad, stressed and disoriented.

I didn't cry. I had no time for tears. I had to focus on getting myself safely out of here. I tapped on the window where the man has been peering in and then hid in the corner. Maybe this way, he'll come and find me, or at least wonder what I was up to. But he didn't come. So, I went to the window, pulled up my top and flashed my breasts. Maybe that would get his attention, but he barely reacted. I know it smacks of desperation, but I am locked up and no one is talking to me. Did they want me to go mad? The waiting was the worst part. I had no idea how long I'd be waiting. I rang the bell again and again. Finally, a harassed-looking woman appeared. I recognised her as the one who was crying while talking to the tall man in the hallway. She was pretty, high-cheekboned, with big, vivid green eyes and a kind face. She had a thick Slavic-sounding accent, possibly Russian or Polish. I concentrated hard on understanding her as she explained something to me. I picked up that I must wait here and I would be taken somewhere else. It seemed like she might care a little about me. But she was impatient, too, telling me off for ringing the buzzer.

After she left, the tall, dark-haired middle-aged guy came into the room with two other older men, all wearing white coats over suits. I asked him if he would hold my thumb. I just needed to feel some contact with another human being. He looked at me and nodded. The warmth of his hand made me feel still connected to the world.

The other two men looked officious. Again, the crushing avalanche of questions about what had happened to me in the past week. With three grown men sitting around my bed, I felt very small and insignificant. Only two weeks, or maybe three, my husband had sat at my bedside to tell me something that unravelled my life. What did these men want from me? I noticed one of them had a French accent. I told them my story, hoping they'd feel pity and let me go. As I recounted, in excruciating detail, what my husband had done and those poor kids who had to be told they weren't going to their new home after all, the French guy became misty-eyed. I saw him wipe away a single tear from his cheek with his sleeve. I did my best to answer their questions and then they left.

Alone again, I sank back into my enormous nest of white sheets. It all felt quite surreal and reminded me of the fairy tale, The Princess and the Pea, sitting in this high up bed. The pretty Slavic woman returned to tell me that I would be leaving the room soon. She and a young guy took me into a lift and up a few floors, then walked me through a maze of corridors. Looking through the windows, I could see the outside world. It was a typically British bleak and grey day. Still a little dazed and disoriented, I was happy to be out of the locked room and be able to stretch my legs.

They took me to a purple room that was much smaller and cosier with a single bed in it. There was a small corner annexe with a tiny moulded, fitted bathroom and shower. They told me to put on a gown with an open back and lie on the bed. I did as I was told. Then four people held me down. One of them was holding a long needle. They were going to inject me with something. There was no getting out of it. In sheer panic, I told them I was pregnant, hoping they would take pity and not poison me with whatever was in that shot.

My husband had asked me a few days before we split up, quite casually, if was I pregnant. That must be where I got the idea to say this. But I wasn't pregnant. They didn't care one way or another and jabbed the needle into my backside. It was over in a flash and I was gone.

12

Day one: Purple Haze

I was once again alone in a new bed in another unfamiliar room. The walls were a shade of violet like a stormy night-time sky. It was as if I was in the middle of a bad acid trip. My head felt like a black hole and my memories were patchy. The last thing I recall was being injected with the needle. I knew I hadn't done anything wrong and there had been some kind of mix up. I was the person wronged, I didn't abandon my children-to-be, my husband did.

My mind flicked back to the day before, retracing the steps of how I wound up here. The last thing I remembered was screaming my head off in the car park and being bundled into an ambulance while Laura and Kelly watched. They had hounded me until they literally pushed me over the edge, so I got thrown into this place. I remembered waking up in that creepy sterile white room and pressing the buzzer. The pissed-off man answering it. He was a black guy, and I woke up in the night worried that they had sent me to Africa where my husband was going to see to it that I would be tortured further.

Where am I now? A proper inmate like in the 80s TV show Prisoner Cell Block H. Lying in my single prison bed and staring at the ceiling, I could see tiny security cameras and that I was being monitored. My every move was being watched. I was wearing a pale-pink nightgown, which was only tied at the back. At least this time I had my own toilet—a massive upgrade. I could have a shower and go to the toilet in my own room. I felt a huge relief and a sense of gratitude for this. Even though I didn't feel safe, it was better than the clinical white goldfish bowl that I was shunted into before.

What do I do now? I searched around my new environment to take a closer look. On the sideboard, I noticed there were my clothes, and handbag, the few belongings I had arrived with.

On the other side of the room, there was an empty closet. The door had a small glass window with slats to the outside, where they could spy on me. I eventually realised the door wasn't locked and walked through it into the corridor that was full of doors the same as mine—like one of those soulless corporate hotels that went on forever. It was quiet and ahead of me, I saw a set of double doors. It opened out into a long, light-filled community room scattered with an array of comfortable sofas and chairs. In one corner, there was a small kitchenette and nearby two doors, one leading to a TV room and another to a consulting room.

My mind flashed back to the night before. I suspected I was in some kind of detention facility. I heard the keys clunking all night long, the slats of my window being opened and closed and the glow of a torchlight shining the bright light into my face. Alone and abandoned, I felt no one cared or noticed why I was missing. All I needed to know was how to fight my way out of there. I needed a new plan. First, find out the rules and then follow them. Again, it occurred to me that I was being tested. And if I passed, maybe I would get my children after all. I just needed to stay alive long enough and things would sort themselves out. I had to keep the faith. I thought about the Dalai Lama and how much compassion and human kindness he had for the world.

Sitting in the open community room, I gazed around at the other women. Some were engrossed in jigsaw puzzles, some colouring in, and others just lounged around chatting. I wandered over to an armchair in the far corner and sat alone, not wanting to intrude on anyone's space. Suddenly I recognised someone that had gone to the same school as me. This can't be possible, can it? I must be seeing lookalikes again. Oh my god, how could they have planted this person from my past in this place?

When I was at my most stressed, I started seeing lookalikes. I knew there are many people we meet who look or remind us of other people we had known. But what was the chance, that when I entered this place, psychiatric hospital or prison, on my first day, I would see someone I knew back at school when I was ten years old in the late-70s? I knew it was her, why was she in my story? Or maybe it was just my mind trying to make sense of this new world. I gazed at the woman, who had quite a distinctive look, mixed-raced and extremely pretty, and tried to remember her name. She had a long frizzy mane of curls framing a heart- shaped face and big brown expressive eyes. She was quite a loner. I wondered how she ended up here. Thinking she must have suffered from some form of anxiety, I felt a sudden guilt.

Maybe the adoption agency had set this up as some sort of trick? A little freaked out, I thought it was best to lie low and hope that this setup and the whole experience in here would go away.

I would spend many days in this communal space or the TV room, lost in a haze of daytime telly and soaps, but had little memory since my brain was foggy with whatever drugs they forced on me. The days and nights blurred into each other. I slipped into their system of being drugged and shepherded around, while all the time hoping and praying for a miracle that would get me out of here.

Inside my violet room, my new routine was to get up, shower and get dressed. Take the drugs, eat, sleep and follow orders. I only had the clothes I was wearing and my handbag. I didn't know where I was, only that I wasn't allowed out. It was very depressing. I did have my own room now and having a bathroom felt like the greatest luxury. I had been upgraded or graduated as a person that could take herself to the bathroom without asking—whatever next. The bathroom was a cubbyhole and, when I looked a little closer,

I realised, like in a prison, there was no toilet seat and the taps could only be turned on, but turned off by themselves. The towels were tiny, just about big enough to dry off a cat, so I couldn't hang myself. I had lost the privilege of being human.

I didn't talk to anyone. I was scared of everyone. Through my bedroom window I could see some workmen working outside on the roof, but they couldn't see me. Something I didn't realise at first. I was in a high-rise building in a city, so no trees or a speck of green to see. There were no plants and nothing felt alive in this place. The window opened only about an inch and the smells of tobacco smoke and fresh tarmac, a toxic combination, drifted into my room and made me feel queasy. They were working on the roof, day after day, and I could hear the incessant sound of drilling and workmen banter. I couldn't cope with those smells in my small room and shut the window tightly.

There was no peace and quiet. I was sure my room was bugged. Like the other cell, there were objects with tiny red blinking lights stuck on the ceiling that looked like cameras and recording devices. I was obviously being monitored 24/7, which fuelled my paranoia and fear. I had nothing to hide, though, all I was doing was sleeping, writing and sometimes drawing. Somehow, in spite of my fuzzy head, I knew it was important to be on my best behaviour.

When the lights went out, the staff, on their nightly suicide-watch rounds, walked past my door with their keys jangling. Every half hour or so, they would slide open the slatted window on the door, shining the light into my face to see if I was still alive. It was frightening to be woken up this way, and continuously throughout the night. Even if I locked my door, the staff had a key, so they could enter, if by some miracle, I was asleep. I kept my door locked, as it felt safer out of the clutches of the other inmates. I just had to hope the staff were decent and not weirdos too.

With the constant checks throughout the night, I found sleeping wasn't an option, which didn't help my anxiety in my drugged-up, fragile mental state. I was scared of the dark, scared of the inmates, and scared of some of the staff. On top of the awfulness and uncertainty of being here, I felt abandoned by my family and everyone in the outside world. Losing control of my life and being ejected from normal society was an indescribable feeling.

My stomach ached constantly, but I was told hot-water bottles weren't allowed. I had to take medication every day, not knowing what I was being given. At night, when I couldn't sleep, I soon realised I wasn't the only one. After dark, the place came alive, with bodies passing through the sterile, haunted corridors like ghosts trapped in between worlds. So, at least, I had some sense of normalcy.

In the first few days, I worked on being invisible, not talking to anyone and minding my own business. The place was very unpredictable and some of my fellow patients/inmates would shock me by randomly shouting abusive language. One inmate, in particular, shot me intimidating looks and out of earshot of the staff, swore at me. Eventually, I told one of the friendlier-looking staff who promised to keep a watchful eye.

I began to fear I was in danger of losing my identity. I had nothing familiar or that was mine to anchor me here. The only clothes I had was, the dress and coat I bought the day I was bundled into that ambulance. I had been given the regulation hospital pink gown, with the slit up the back. At night, I wrapped myself in a white flannel dressing gown they had lent me to go to sleep. It made me feel like I wasn't even worthy of something decent to wear.

During the first four days, I was allowed to visit the shop and buy a pair of second-hand corduroy jeans and a jacket for just 50p. It was surreal, like a sketch from a sitcom, finding this little make-believe shop in the hospital. Oh, look here's a patient coming into the shop, let's put the OPEN sign up and let them in.

Inside the place, a cross between a prison and a hospital, I had lost all control of my life and was acutely sensitive to everything.

Added to this, I was being pumped full of drugs and lived in perpetual fear. I was in survival mode, clinging onto a routine and biding my time to make it out of this grim institution, whatever it was.

It was a noisy hectic place, with buzzers and alarms going off all the time. I had no idea what the alarms meant and why the staff would go running around the place, looking for someone or something. It was only much later that I realised people were actually trying to kill themselves.

We, the patients/inmates, would spend all day queuing either to see the doctor for meds or just to be able to talk to a member of staff. Sometimes you would wait all day long and still not be seen. The staff were changing shifts at least three times a day and weren't paid enough to care. I tried to keep a low profile. The head honcho, a tall, handsome Swedish guy, who everyone said was lovely and helpful, only worked three or four days a week.

The daily routine 7:30 am queue for meds, then to breakfast by 8:30 am. The canteen looked like a shabbier, more institutional version of a school cafeteria with a line for hot food and a scattering of long communal tables. The men from the nearby ward would also be having their breakfast. It meant I had more people to avoid. I would first collect a tray and have porridge or toast and a cup of tea or coffee and sit in the farthest, loneliest corner of the room, where I could avoid eye contact but not too far from the staff in case a fight broke out. The other patients looked in a bad way, zombie-like and groggy from all the drugs, especially the men.

Treating us like violent, disturbed schoolkids, a group of staff was constantly observing everyone in the canteen to make sure no one got into any trouble. They would write down what you were doing or how you appeared. I later found out they called it OBS or observations.

After breakfast,I'd return to my room but needed a staff member to unlock my door. Sometimes this took a while since they were overwhelmed and overworked. I made sure I was always patient and kind to them, not wanting to fall out with anyone in case they took revenge on me.

Again, we'd gather for lunch at 12:30 pm and dinner at 5:30 pm. Then 7 pm it was time to queue for meds before bedtime. No counselling, although we were allocated a support worker for each of the three shifts a day. The support worker was supposed to have a three-minute chat with you during the shift to check you were okay. I don't recall that ever happening much to me. They just observed me and wrote something down on their clip board. I kept to myself and wrote in my journals every day, and sometimes I would make a drawing of my room to pass the endless stretch of time.

13

Drugs Don't Work

Every afternoon I would queue up in the long line around the building and take whatever drugs I was given, like a good patient. In line, I avoided eye contact with anyone and disappeared into my own world. Enjoying the feel of sunlight on my face pouring in from the large windows, I would close my eyes and pretend I was outside. I really missed nature. Just like in One Flew Over the Cuckoo's Nest, we would stand opposite the dispensary hatch door and be given a paper cup with water in it and the pills to swallow. In the evening, after dinner, we would queue up again to receive our drugs.

After taking my night-time pill, I would head to my cubbyhole room and write about my day and my thoughts. One evening I woke up in the dead of the night, feeling nauseous, my heart racing. I slowly built up the strength to drag myself out of bed and ask for help. I went to the staff room and said I felt sick and I was given a sick bowl by the nurse and taken back to my room. I told her I was struggling to breathe and needed some oxygen. I thought I was going to have a heart attack.

One nurse came into my room and saw me, and she left. I was starting to feel like I was dying. I didn't want to die. I grabbed my pen and a piece of paper on my bedside table and told myself, "I will write", so I wrote, I am alive, I am alive. It reassured me that by writing I was still here. I kept writing throughout the night. I dated it and wrote the time as proof of what I was experiencing. Otherwise, no one would believe me.

Luckily, I had some notebooks. Marcus had kept telling me to write everything down as evidence. I knew it was the drugs they were giving me. So I started to write to try and prevent myself from panicking and to stay calm:

1.33 am—Panic attack—rapid heartbeat—side effects. Cramp in my foot; panic—the lights are too bright. Drug sensitivity—my heart hurts. I drew outlines of hearts within hearts on the paper. Symbolising my heart, which felt like it was juddering in my chest. Danger— panic attack. Someone help me!

I struggled to get up, but managed by slowly easing myself off the bed. I knew this was only going to get worse and had to find someone to help. I didn't want to die and feel all this pain alone. There were a couple of people on night duty. I saw an Irish woman called Theresa, but couldn't talk since I was having trouble breathing. So instead I wrote a note and showed it to her.

Glancing at it, she said, "I can't read it."

Theresa was the support worker on duty, alongside another nurse. They both looked at me with blank, glazed expressions as though I was bothering them. Maybe I was but this breathlessness and immense pain shooting through my chest seemed quite real to me. They just stared at me—unbothered and bloody useless. I went back to my room, carefully lying down in my nest of sheets. I was either going to get through this or die.

Half-sat up in bed, I wrote the best I could: 1.37 am—Rapid heartbeat—my heart hurts—no oxygen—no pressure (meaning no one has taken my blood pressure). I continued to scribble in my notepad at least by doing this I knew I was still alive. 1.42 am—panic— noisy ventilation unit. 1.50 am—rapid heart rate.

I drew hearts within hearts, feeling the pen on the paper. I knew I was still here. I pressed the alarm. Switched the light on and off as some sort of SOS signal. Still, no one came. I continued to write in the pre-dawn darkness until daylight arrived through my window.

After showering and getting dressed, I went back to the same nurse on duty, Theresa and told her, "I had a massive panic attack last night and you didn't help me."

"I didn't notice," she replied and stomped off as though I offended her.

What kind of a place was this?

That night I had filled 20 pages of my lovely new book. I'd become a little obsessed with stationary lately. I was now writing and drawings every day—the only way to survive this place.

The first time I ever experienced a panic attack was after my band toured Japan. Somehow we got through an exhausting tour without any drama. On the plane ride back on 16 January 1995, I made a trip to the bathroom and while in there my heart started thumping loudly, like it was bouncing off the walls of the confined space. The air hostess suggested I stay seated until the plane emptied out. I eventually walked off the plane. At home, between jetlag and exhaustion, I shook my boyfriend awake in the middle of the night and told him I was dying tomorrow and just wanted to let him know. Luke, with his mop of strawberry blonde hair, flicked on the light and asked what was going on. I had felt my body enlarging and becoming very small, apparently delirium. He assured me I was having a bad dream and we went back to sleep. The next morning the Kobe earthquake happened, and we were in shock. I went to the doctor and was diagnosed with nervous exhaustion.

Now nearly 20 years later, the day after my panic attack in the psychiatric hospital, I was furious the duty nurse just dismissed me. I was drained and depleted but determined to see the head psychiatrist, the Swedish chap who, according to everyone, was so lovely. Since it was still very early in the morning, I was first in the queue. I sat patiently waiting to be called. It was my first time seeing him. I sat down at a huge table, opposite the Swedish doctor, flanked by two nurses. All eyes were on me.

I refused to be intimidated by their formality and told the head psychiatrist, "Last night, I had a massive panic attack. My heart rate was beating off the scale and I could barely breathe. I know it's due to the drugs I'd been given. Can my prescription be lowered?"

The Swede listened, leaned in, and said, "Take the drugs and find a sympathetic nurse."

"Really? Last night I asked two nurses for help and neither were sympathetic."

"You can go now."

So Dr Stephan was more than happy for me to have killer panic attacks every night, and all I needed was to find a sympathetic nurse who clearly didn't exist in this place. I was shocked by his lack of compassion. I was only being reasonable I thought. There was no point in talking to these people, who might listen, but nothing changed. Dr Stephan was supposed to be a lovely, helpful person.

That was a bit of a crazy day. Everyone else who went in and saw the head honcho, Dr Stephan, came out crying. I didn't, of course. I'd had enough and knew I had to start standing up for myself since no one else was going to.

Weirdly, virtually every staff member was called a support worker. Aside from drugging and overdosing me to the point of serious panic attacks, I hadn't been given any support in the whole ridiculous, rule-obsessed setup. They were hardly Support Workers. Petty and mean, they were obsessed with writing OBVS or 'observations' about the inpatients. They forced drugs on us, carried keys to open our rooms and allowed a chosen few to sometimes access the outside world. They were useless wankers who seemed to enjoy wielding power over our sad little lives.

Nothing was wrong with me. I was just deeply depressed and heartbroken. My diagnosis was called GRIEF. In a fury, I wrote down my list:

- Loss of husband after an affair
- Loss of children due to loss of husband
- Loss of home
- Loss of privacy

- Violation of my body and soul
- Abandoned by my family
- Betrayed and sectioned
- No fucking access to my friends (I did this to protect my friends, not wanting to burden them).

I was the one suffering. I had been mistreated and dumped in this loony bin where I was cut off from the world and barely existed as a human being. Now I had to meet with a panel of people to decide whether or not I could leave this terrible dump of a place, where I had been sleep-deprived and drugged up to my eyeballs. Which, in the end, did nothing but worsen my anxiety and fragile mental state. There was no peace for me.

I knew once I got out I was going to leave this grim, gloomy island, away from Andy, away from Helen and all the people who ruined my life. More than anything, I needed a place to heal. An Indian ashram sounded appealing. Maybe a Buddhist retreat. I would discuss this with Dr Misra, the only sympathetic doctor working at the unit. I needed to sort out my mobile phone so I could ask my sister Kathy, who was living in Nepal, for advice.

I had to ask for a day off to see my lawyer and start divorce proceedings. I couldn't cope with being locked up and being force-fed drugs. One way or another they seemed determined to kill me, if not physically, then killing my spirit. Again, I was living, or existing, in One Flew Over the Cuckoo's Nest. I felt like the silent Native American guy who rarely spoke but had enormous strength and could bulldoze myself out of here. Maybe this place is teaching me something. Maybe I must learn what it's like to really suffer.

There was an atmosphere in the community room that day, a lot of anxiety as the patients had to wait around all day to see 'the lovely' Swedish head psychiatrist. I didn't think he was lovely at all, but an inflexible, inhumane tosser. You couldn't get a time slot to see him, but just had to wait around all day and feeling more and more anxious while waiting. I could feel the heavy atmosphere in the place—all the angry and anxious women practically tearing their hair out.

Well, that day it hit a crescendo. The woman who had gone around verbally assaulting everyone went up to a young teenage girl and attempted to strangle her. Oh my God. I was in a nearby room at the time, with a staff member, as I had been stressed out by this psychotic woman. They were out of sight, but I could hear the noise of the girl grasping for breath. Luckily she was saved by another patient and the police were called. The aggressive woman was removed from the unit. The poor girl whom she tried to strangle was visibly shaking and you could see the deep-purple bruising on her neck. I felt sorry for this girl, who was softly spoken and seemed like such a sweet spirit, and was likely more traumatised than when she came here. I felt lucky she hadn't attacked me. Only the day before, she screeched at me, calling me "a fucking cruel and heartless bitch" and accusing me of taking away her children. Little did she know I'd had my would-be adopted children snatched away.

My blood pressure shot up even more since that woman had verbally assaulted me. I couldn't bear being around her and the staff said they would look after me. From that day onwards, they insisted on taking my blood pressure every day.

There were so many rules, all to protect everyone from killing themselves. No glass of any kind or, if you had a bottle of something, it had to be locked up in another cupboard within your room. I, on the other hand, may have hated my life but wasn't tired of living and had never had any intention of killing myself. The Crisis at Home woman had asked me that. And, ironically, here I was surrounded by 19 women who were all suicidal. Why wasn't I just put in a rehab facility, somewhere I would be cared for instead of being shut away and dehumanised?

My husband had created this god-almighty mess. All the dominoes were stacked up and, with one flick, they had all fallen down on me. The social worker, at the adoption agency, was incredibly unsupportive and seemed to blame me for the sorry state of affairs. My sister who had me sectioned didn't even call or visit.

As the initial shock of my terrifying new environment waned, I became obsessed with getting out. But how? As a child, my worst fear was being wrongly sent to prison. Now I was in a kind of prison. This whole experience made me feel worthless. I felt physically violated by the fact I had been married to that man whom I had loved and trusted and who didn't give a damn about me or the wreckage he left behind. Why had I not seen the signs—the screaming red-alert signals that seemed obvious to everyone else? Why had I constantly made excuses for him, blaming his cruel behaviour on the stress of the adoption, crushing workload and all his work in schools for children in the whole of bloody Africa? Why had I trusted this devious fraud and emotional retard? I remembered a conversation I had the very last time I heard his voice. I called up the school to speak to the head and had accidentally been put through to him. All he said in a cold, flat voice was "Alice, what do you want?" I repeated, "I wanted to speak to the head, and you're not the head", and slammed the phone down.

One day we had the option of meditation with the psychologist and I jumped at the chance. A tall, slender and attractive woman in her 30s, she looked quite sophisticated in her well-cut navy suit and white silk top. She sat down in the middle of her pink and purple sofa. Only one other person came along and that was Phyllis Danes, the girl I went to school with. The girl I imagined was actually her. How strange that we would both end up in this place at the same time. I later found out that she had been intimidating other people in the unit, by talking aggressively to them. She hadn't said a word to me though and blanked me. Obviously, we were all here for different reasons and it wasn't my business to nose into why she was here. I later found out that, as mad as it sounded to me, some people came here and checked themselves in voluntarily. The terrible irony of it. All I wanted to do was get out. This seemed impossible since I was sectioned. I just wanted someone to listen to me, but no one could be bothered. The only thing they did was drug us. After the strangulation episode, the other women all started to chat a bit and I met some very nice and intelligent suicidal people.

One day, when I was trying to use the computer to check my emails on these ridiculous old PC dinosaurs that were stuck to the wall, I saw a man who wore a vicar's collar walk through the community room. I had noticed the chaplaincy room, but he was never in. Here right in front of me was a real live chaplain. I didn't care what religion he was, I just needed to speak to someone vaguely normal and hopefully empathetic.

I asked if I could speak to him and he took me into the chaplaincy room. I started to tell him about the heartbreak of losing my adopted children, the shock of being sectioned and, amazingly, he actually listened. After a full hour, he said he had to go, but reassured me he would pray for me.

During my stay in the hospital, when I woke up, I showered, got dressed, put on make- up and got ready for the day. A lot of the women didn't bother and languished, unwashed and dishevelled, in their dressing gowns all day long. I tried to have some sort of routine and purpose in this holding pad until I would be allowed to leave. I wrote every day, despite being heavily drugged. Later I found out they had misdiagnosed me and were treating me for bipolar disorder.

14

Lost and Found

On 21 October, four days after my arrival, I had a surprise visit from Sara. I wasn't forgotten after all and I still existed in some form or another. Most of the time I walked around peacefully, trying to gather information about this place and figure out how it all worked. I observed people's behaviour and discreetly watched them interact. I was observed by the staff throughout the day, so I, too, observed them. I had ultra-high blood pressure and could feel my mind speeding and panicking at any perceived threat or danger. I wasn't aware that I had high blood pressure at this point and assumed I was just losing my mind.

The day before I was called to the community room and told I had a phone call from my sister Sara. I was a bit confused, but at last, someone was connecting with me. Since I no longer had a phone, I went to find the phone booth in the lounge area. I hadn't noticed it before. It was a communal phone in a small cramped alcove. I entered the makeshift booth and picked up the phone, my mind in a bit of a daze. It felt claustrophobic and uncomfortably hot. I ended up using it quite a lot, so it kind of became my own personal phone box. Everyone else seemed to have a mobile, except for me—their own lifeline out of this place. The annoying thing about the phone box was that I had to stand and take a call and not move an inch since the lead was ridiculously short. Much later I realised it was short so no one could strangle themselves. Of course, this never entered my head. I just wanted to get out of there alive.

Sara had managed to make contact after I had been drugged up in the unit for at least four days. It was the policy of the unit that she had to ask my permission for a visit. So she called and asked if I wanted to see her. "Yes, of course, please come," I told her, without sounding too desperate. I had felt abandoned by everyone else.

Sara, my very first visitor, arrived at 4 pm that afternoon. Since being admitted I had suffered acute panic attacks and feared for my life living among some of the volatile inmates. I was sleep-deprived and what little sleep I had was solely drug-induced. Between the unsettling noises and flashing torches at night and my persistent stomach pain, I was as together as could be expected.

Sara, casually dressed in blue jeans and a pretty white top, plonked herself down on a sofa in the community room. She sat there staring up at me, while I looked bewildered by seeing a real person who knew me and my story. I was also a little pissed off that my family, or rather my sister Laura, would have me locked up knowing what had happened to me.

Sara brought along a suitcase full of my clothes and I was excited. Aside from a few bits I bought in the hospital charity shop, I'd been wearing the same clothes that I arrived in. Seeing Sara in the flesh stirred up some difficult feelings. I was still furious and didn't understand why I was imprisoned in this loony bin and abandoned by everyone else. I had noticed other people got visitors daily and were allowed out while I was stuck inside. I felt an incredible sense of failure, losing my personal freedom. And suddenly I was thrust back to a semblance of normality seeing my sweet, caring sister in my new controlled environment.

Sara was drained and frazzled by the whole shitty situation. Having made a three-hour journey, she had picked up the suitcase from Laura's house on the way down from Surrey. I could see the deep sadness in her big, brown eyes. She didn't need to say a word, as her tender, open face gazed at me with the love of a close sibling.

She had been the one who had shared the deepest and darkest nights with me.

Now she looked up at me and saw the new robotic emptiness that I inhabited. I had surrendered under a haze of punishing drugs forced on me. I was resigned to standing in line like a zombie, ready to receive the toxic drug of their choice, like everyone else. If I hadn't been so dazed and partly checked out, I would've hugged my sister. Instead, I stared at her, groggy and uncommunicative.

She studied my face cautiously and asked, "How are you doing?"

"Terrible," I told her flat out. "I have no idea why I'm here, Sara. I'm surrounded by nutters and I'm not like them. I don't belong here."

"I'm sorry, Alice. I don't understand why you're here either."

"I don't feel safe here. One particular woman is really aggressive and nasty and scares me." I looked at her pleadingly on the cusp of tears. "This is like a concentration camp. I'll do anything to get out... anything."

"I'll do whatever I can, Alice," she said and recounted the herculean effort it had been just to find me. "I'm not giving up on you."

I didn't quite understand what she meant in my dazed and drugged state. I felt her every unexpressed emotion and found it hard to bear.

Sara quietly opened the suitcase. I rummaged through expecting to see my clothes and then freaked out.

"There's hardly anything of mine in here," I said irritably, upset and confused about how she could bring me a suitcase full of clothes that weren't mine. This was yet another sign that I wasn't even worthy of having my own clothes.

"This is what Laura gave me and told me was yours."

"Well, most of this isn't mine," I said, distressed, throwing a pile of clothes back in the suitcase. "Can you lend me some cash so I can buy some clothes at least?"

She didn't look too happy with my erratic behaviour and stroppiness. But since I was stuck in this miserable place, I didn't think it was unreasonable to want to wear my own clothes. My sensitivity and what she perceived as an overreaction confused my sister. She gave me some cash and said she would get me a phone. After taking a few items of clothes I recognised, she left and I shuffled back to my room.

At least I would have some kind of contact with the outside world again. As if I wasn't under enough stress already, my blood pressure shot up to around 180.

Somehow I endured the daily misery of this place by going around minding my own business, sticking to my routine of shower, drugs and sitting in my room writing in between meals. It was like living in another universe, some strange alternate reality. I would go to the canteen for breakfast and discreetly watch the people in there. I would slowly and mindfully eat my food. I noticed one man was wearing a woman's dress. Like me, most people just wanted to be left alone. I watched the men, who could barely put food in their mouths. My God, they were in a bad way. I tried to stay positive and told myself that this was just a mistake and it would be rectified soon.

Every night before going to bed, I made sure I locked my room, afraid of what might happen to me during the night. As a child I'd always been afraid of the dark. In this place, I was afraid of everything. An 'asylum' by definition was supposed to be a place of safety, but the word triggered terrifying cultural associations in the vein of One Flew Over the Cuckoo's Nest, Shutter Island or Girl, Interrupted—the brutal treatment of patients, the electric shock therapy, the murders and unmarked graves through the centuries. And I had plenty of reasons to be fearful, particularly from some of the crazed, aggressive women, drugged off their heads, roaming and rambling on in the corridors. Not to mention the ever-changing staff and vague and shifting rules. One rule was not to tell you very much, leaving you in the dark to work it out for yourself. Some rules I knew were: you had to use your own toilet, so that meant someone had to unlock your door. You had to find a member of staff to help you and ask them politely to open your door to use the loo. Hunting down staff in a stressful and understaffed environment became a part-time job in itself. I just stayed in my room so that I had autonomy over my toilet trips and could avoid the other inmates.

One day in the common room, I noticed a huge notice board, pinned with various leaflets with lots of complicated, unpronounceable names on it. These were the drugs we were all taking. The leaflet explained what each drug was for and how it could help you. I was horrified to see all the drugs people were on. I assumed we were supposed to just find a drug we thought would help and ask for it. Although I found out it didn't work like that—it was an information service to tell you more about the drug that had been prescribed for you. Thinking about that, I realised that no one had told me what my condition was? Much later I found out there was a book with guidelines in it that they were supposed to give you on arrival, but predictably I never received it.

As soon as I got in here, I wanted to flee. After a while, I realised if I were to survive this ordeal I had better play along.

One gloomy, drizzly late-October afternoon, a few days after Sara's visit, she came back with Marcus. Thrilled to see familiar faces again it gave me a shard of hope. The two of them spoke to the head psychiatrist and told him I was sane, if a little grief-stricken and depressed, and asked about releasing me. That was when we found out that I had been officially sectioned under the 136 Mental Health Act and put on a 28-day section. Which meant no one, not even my family, could get me off this. Not that anyone else seemed bothered by my disappearance from the world. I imagined most people thought I would be with my newly adopted children, getting to know them. Instead I was doped up and shut away in a psych ward on a section.

Apparently, I had first, been detained on a '136' isolation in that white room—even though I had seen the Crisis at Home people who agreed I wasn't in any danger to myself or others. Now I was on a 'section 3', which meant being held against my will for 28 bloody days, and I hadn't even had a diagnosis.

I could understand that there were perfectly valid reasons behind involuntary hospitalisation—primarily if a mentally unstable person is unable to make good choices for themselves or if they were psychotic and dangerous, but I wasn't any of those things. Oh well, at least I knew I wouldn't be stuck in this terrible, soul-sapping place forever.

After speaking with the head, Marcus found out the only way off my section was to go to a tribunal and appeal to a panel of people who then had the authority to remove me from the fixed-date section. This was a bit of a conundrum. Since I was sectioned it meant I wasn't allowed outside of the building, unless I had a visitor, in which case I would be allowed out for a couple of hours a day. So, basically, I had 22 or 24 hours a day locked up in a dreary high-rise tower. There was a small outside space on the roof, where inmates would smoke, under supervision.

Shockingly, most of the patients were here on a voluntarily basis. Those that checked themselves in could leave at any time. I, on the other hand, was trapped. It made me think of the words to the Eagle's song Hotel California, 'you can check out any time you like, but you can never leave.'

During the day we were encouraged to do jigsaws and colour in pictures from books as though we were children. I hated doing jigsaws and I hadn't used a colouring book since Primary School. I preferred to sort out crucial paperwork to start rebuilding my life. The only thing that kept me sane was doodling and writing endlessly in my journal.

That afternoon, Marcus, Sara and I stood by the reception desk, where all the information about the drugs was held. Marcus came across a course leaflet called WRAP (Wellness Recovery Action Plan). It was a four-day course that would help me in the future and go some way towards being released sooner than the 28 days. I immediately filled in the form, which needed posting—bizarrely we aren't allowed just to hand it in there. What I didn't know when I applied was that the letter was returned to my home address, three months later, stamped 'address unknown'. This was some messed-up scenario.

Whatever I needed to do at this stage seemed like another game I was forced to play. Together, Marcus and I tried to lodge my appeal against my sectioning and were told this would take a few weeks. This Byzantine bureaucracy was obscene. All the crazy catch-22 rules seemed to be designed to break your spirit and make you go mad if you weren't already. My only option was to play this stupid game of the draconian system and be nice to the 'support' workers who literally held the keys to everything in my shrunken universe. They were constantly watching me and taking notes, intensifying my paranoia. Some were nicer than others. Burnt-out and tired, they were going through the motions of babysitting a herd of unstable, over-emotional people, silent depressives and schizophrenics having full-on hallucinations and violent outbursts. I tried not to take it personally and counted the interminable days when I could leave.

Having a lot of time to kill, I holed up in my room, number 4.04, which had a large grey solid door and looked like a regulation prison cell door that I'd seen on TV and in films. It had a smaller square window, with slats that opened from the outside, so at any point, someone could pop their head and look in, usually at night but sometimes during the day too. It was the support worker's job to keep tabs on us to make sure everyone was alive and behaving. I suppose they saw it as protecting inpatients from themselves, but I felt as though I needed protection from them. Each shift, another set of people arrived to stare and observe you like you were some strange exotic insect under a microscope. I couldn't keep track of who was assigned to me.

I found the number 4.04 a reoccurring theme. A bit disturbingly, I got married on 4.4.2009. It felt like a reminder of my doomed marriage and the reason I was here after all. On day one I was injected with an unknown drug and knocked out until the next day. The following days I was drugged on Quetiapine, 100mcg in the morning and 100mcg in the evening. I didn't know this at the time but Quetiapine is given to people with psychosis, schizophrenia and bipolar disorder—and it can be taken in high doses up to 800mcg.

I was still waking up at 4 am since sleeping was impossible. Here, like when I was at home, I was restless and manic. Maybe in some subconscious way, it reminded me of that day when everything in my life suddenly collapsed. So I would get up and roam the corridors or wander into the community room, find an empty sofa and sleep on it. Somehow a sofa felt safer than a bed and being in a communal space with other zombies than alone in my locked cell, where I was being watched and monitored.

Room 404 was my cell where I was going to spend the next three weeks. Over and over, I kept thinking about what had I done wrong to be incarcerated. When I stopped obsessing about my sad situation, I realised everyone here was in a bad way. I discovered that all 19 of the other women, even the ones who were here voluntarily, had tried to commit suicide. Some had even tried multiple times. I had no intention of killing myself or hurting others, so the great mystery was why I was being held against my will for being heartbroken and depressed.

Around 2 am, the evening after Sara and Marcus visited, I woke up from a dream, where I was creating a fantasy future of forgiving my husband and still being able to adopt the children that were matched to us. I was sane after all and my husband was teaching in a school so was surely okay. Andy could return to me, once he gets his mind sorted. He said he wasn't having an affair, but just had "feelings for her". He was overworked and under pressure, once he has regained his sanity, maybe we could get back together. Or, by some miracle, if I could adopt on my own, the children and I could live in Dorset and my mum, sisters and family friends nearby could help me.

Half-asleep, I grabbed my notebook and drifted into the community room. I made myself a camomile tea and started to write about the ward and the people I had met. Some were nice and others particularly nasty and likely had troubled and abuse-ridden lives. The woman who kept attacking people had her children taken off her.

I kept scribbling ideas. My thoughts kept wandering to beautiful places. In one dream, Andy took six months off work and we went to Nepal and India. We lived in an ashram and he found the inner beauty in his soul that was buried deep inside of him. Underneath the cocky exterior, he was just an insecure boy lacking in confidence and his soul being crushed by the ridiculous demands of modern society and state schooling. Maybe he just couldn't cope and found comfort in Helen, his best friend and lover, who didn't ask about his feelings. We would eventually be a wonderful, caring family. Maybe we could move to Dorset and that would be a place to rejuvenate our soul family.

When I woke up with a jolt, I was in my room, locked up, the bad dream hadn't faded away. Getting up, I fell into my daily rhythm: shower, dress, put on makeup, off to get meds and then breakfast. I had to go through the motions and not show any emotion—inside I felt anger and the injustice. Otherwise, they would probably drug me even more. I was at the mercy of others, so had to surrender to the place and, the people and be grateful for any visitors. I was getting the hang of this place.

15

Derailed but undefeated

In the second week, my patience slipped, I had reached the point beyond what I could endure. Being locked up 24/7, the place made me claustrophobic and afraid for my well-being. Knowing there wasn't a hope in hell of leaving sooner, I was desperate to get out for my two-hour daily break. I had things to do, I had to get a divorce and get my life back on track.

Totally unexpectedly, Kelly came to visit one evening after work. I had forgiven her for that terrible day and for what she and Laura had done to me. She showed up with John for support. When they arrived, they looked startled and uneasy, like a pair of woodland creatures caught in headlights. They were watching me cautiously, probably worried about how I would react. I suspected that was why Kelly brought her husband along in case I flipped out. She obviously didn't trust me anymore. And I certainly didn't trust her, but needed a visitor to get me out for of this high-rise hellhole.

I needed to go to the Apple store and sort out something on my iPad since it wouldn't sync properly. I needed to email people. I hadn't told any of my friends about the disastrous ending to my marriage and the loss of my children. A few days earlier, Marcus and I had purchased the iPad at the Apple store together on a previous two-hour getaway and had been in a hurry. As there was no Wi-Fi in a psychiatric unit, I had to buy an iPad with data access since I had no phone. The staff at the store had been so lovely and sorted me out quickly.

So Kelly and John took me back to the Apple store. Afterwards, the three of us went upstairs to the John Lewis Cafe for tea. On the top floor, the café had wraparound windows showing the best views of Southampton Harbour. I could tell Kelly and John found me hard work. No doubt I was being bossy and overbearing since this was my only chance to get anything done. Still, I couldn't help but feel sad that my oldest friend of 45 years didn't have the compassion to look beyond the way I was behaving. Instead, on the car journey to the see the pychiatrist, she told me that a friend of hers had been in there and "it did her a world of good." I had no idea how this place could do me a world of good.

Maybe for my family and friend, I was no longer their responsibility. I called Kelly for help and she sided with my sister and got me sectioned. I know I appeared a bit mad and erratic, but beneath the surface, I just needed a safe place to rest and recover. Both Kelly and Laura wanted me fixed and out of the way. They got what they wanted and here I was shunted away in my own little cell.

Regardless of what my husband had done—a triple fucking whammy—the betrayal of a lying, thieving philanderer, losing those longed-for beautiful children and telling me he didn't want them when I was barely conscious. That last element alone pushed me over the edge into another world. Whenever I was outside, I was thinking, "Fuck him, I'll get over this and I'll survive." Once I was back in the bug house, I felt lost, isolated and fucked up. I was grateful that Kelly came to visit and allowed me a glimpse of the outside world, where I could do normal things.

Marcus and Sara were offering their support again, but they didn't have to live in this sterile, controlling place being doped and caged. Some mornings I'd wake up, after a few hours of sleep, and I couldn't believe I had ended up here. I know everyone did what they thought was best, with the knowledge they had at the time, but still, it was fucking outrageous. It was particularly sad that they didn't offer the compassion and understanding I needed.

As I learned since having therapy, I "had a normal reaction to an abnormal situation". It's funny how no one around me saw it that way. Most people only see the surface of you and the circumstances and didn't have the ability to see beyond that. If I had just cried all the time and stayed in bed all day that would have been more manageable and they may have acted more sympathetically towards me. Sadly for me, I went around reassuring everyone around me instead of actually helping myself. What a enormous lesson to have learned so late in life: to think of oneself before others.

While I was grateful that Kelly came and visited me for those two-hours of freedom, I felt our future friendship probably wouldn't recover or grow from this experience. I had learnt some big lessons about myself and our relationship since we were five years old. I knew I would have to shed and re-examine all of my friendships. In these desperate situations, you really learn who cares about you.

Marcus, Stephanie and Sara all came together one day and took me to what would become my new temporary daytime home, the John Lewis café. We drove up to the shopping centre, with its bright lights and consumerism, probably not the greatest place to have a temporary home, but it was uplifting to be free from the unit and breathe fresh air. I had lost the borrowed dressing gown, so Sara and Stephanie bought me a soft white one with stars on it. It was super soft, and I would wrap myself in it and feel loved wrapped within the soft texture of my skin.

That afternoon the conversation turned to how I was going to be released from the psychiatric ward. They told me to talk slowly, but I found it difficult. Sara had been impressed with me and said I appeared normal. Since the big overnight panic attack, I wasn't on the medication, so I felt much better. Maybe things would start to improve now.

On another visit soon after, Sara brought her husband Dan to see me too. She was excited to show him, now that I was off the meds, that I'd returned to my normal self, sort of. Just before they arrived, one of the support workers took me into her office. I thought it was to see how I was doing. They were supposed to have a five-minute chat with you during each shift, which rarely happened to me. Instead, she berated me for refusing my meds, handed me the pills and insisted that I show her I had swallowed them. It was true I didn't want to take the pills, so yesterday I'd spat out the pill and hid it in a piece of paper. When I rose from the chair, I could feel the drug filtering through my veins, slowly pulling me down and weakening me.

As soon as I walked out of her office, Sara and Dan showed up to whisk me out for some fresh air and freedom. They had driven from Surrey, a good two-and-half- hour journey. I asked Sara to carry my handbag, which suddenly felt as heavy as lead. I told Sara and Dan that I had been drugged and was feeling weak and woozy. We slowly walked down through the park. I remembered how much I enjoyed seeing the trees, I missed seeing the colours of nature, greens, blues, yellows and browns. The leaves were falling and I loved to kick my feet amongst them. It made me feel happy to be outside the high-rise building.

Afterwards, when we got to my new favourite hangout, the John Lewis café, I was exhausted and washed out. I slumped at the table, barely able to hold my head up or pick up my coffee cup—the drug had sapped all my energy. I pulled out a tablet in a piece of paper and gave it to Dan to get rid of it for me. I told them the drugs had been killing me, shooting up my blood pressure and giving me small heart attacks. My sister looked at me with tears in her eyes. She just couldn't believe this was the same person she saw the other day.

So exhausted and weak, I found it difficult to speak and slurred like a drunk. The drug had taken over my body and wrecked me. Sara and Dan took me back after I had bought more perfect-bound notebooks and pens. Writing was fuelling my sanity and the only thing keeping me going. I didn't know this at the time but when we returned, Sara demanded to see the duty manager and asked how they could just drug me like that in the middle of the day, and how I had transformed from just the day before. They didn't seem to care. They could pretty much do whatever they liked and the head seemed to turn a blind eye.

While inside I had acted my way through my time there. It was the only way of coping from day to day with confinement. I kept myself to myself, but after the attempted strangulation of that girl, we inmates united a bit. I met some other people and found out their stories. Since most were here voluntarily, no one could believe I had been sectioned. Yet, ironically, I was the only one who hadn't been suicidal. There appeared to be no talk therapy in there. The only people who did chat were the cleaners, or the domestic goddesses as they called themselves, who were friendly, open and good fun. So I retold them my pathetic story and they listened.

One day I was in the main community room, laughing and chatting to with the domestic goddesses, and a staff member cut me down dead, giving me a telling-off for talking to them. You needed to have a good laugh to endure this depressing atmosphere and the heaviness of anxiety and stress. The fact that we weren't allowed to be happy or chat like normal people was disturbing. Those cleaners and a couple of others who brought a little lightness and levity were my saving grace in there.

There was a lovely young woman, Jess, who was one of the few caring support workers. When I had problems with my bank, she sat beside me being silently supportive, while I called them on the phone. My mind was on overdrive and had been for two weeks. I spoke a lot and desperately felt the need to be heard. The only way I could release things was by writing about everything and drawing, which I did pretty much non-stop.

They liked to do calming activities, like jigsaw puzzles or colouring in, a staff member sometimes played the guitar or if you were lucky you could go into the art therapy room. One day I wandered into the community art room and asked Jess, the friendly support worker, if I could join in. I was feeling very low. It would've been Alfie's second birthday and I should've been having fun with him and being his mother. Instead I was stuck in a mental ward, lost and bereft.

When I sat down in the art room, they were making Halloween paintings. I asked Jess for permission to paint what I wanted since we had to ask permission for everything. I painted a heart made up of layers of beautiful gold and bronze colours and on one side of the heart, there were black dashes like tears. It was the love I felt for Alfie—each of the strokes symbolised all the love and devotion I felt towards this small child, whom I had never met but loved. As I painted, the grief flooded out of me and tears fell from my eyes. I sat in silent meditation painting layers on layers of paint into the metallic heart in front of me. It was my heart. The heart that pumped too much, overflowing with love. The heart that clattered like teacups. The heart that was pumping blood and life into me every day I was alive. I sat alone in my grief. No one asked if I was okay. No one needed to ask since no one could help me. This wasn't a counselling session, but a fun painting session. Alfie was lost forever, and I would never touch my son and say happy birthday.

The patient who sat opposite me in the art room was Phyllis, the pretty mixed-race girl I had been at school with. She was painting her Halloween things and chatting happily to the guy beside her. But she just ghosted me as if I didn't exist.

I plucked up the courage to talk to her. "Hi Phyllis, I don't know if you remember but I went to the same school as you—"

"We don't talk about our personal lives here," she clipped back at me and turned away. Oh, that told me. A good job too, she was probably going to be funny towards me anyway. I did wonder what had happened to her and how she ended up in this place. I would never find out. It was best to keep a low profile and be invisible.

As I sat painting, I told Mark, another support worker, that it was my would-be adoptive son's birthday today and he would've been two. I could see he had misty eyes. I had tears too as I painted a heart for the little boy, whom I'd never see or be his mother. The pain went deep, the loss, sadness and loneliness I felt. I guess I was not only grieving this child, but the crushing realisation that I would never be a mother. I was also trapped in this place without love, completely devastated. At this point, I still thought if I could prove to the adoption agency I was 'good enough' they might let me be the mother to those children.

Afterwards, I went back to my cell, crashed and cried myself to sleep. No one could take this away from me. The feelings of loss were all I had left.

That was the only time I cried in there.

16

A New Way of Seeing

I was a nervous wreck the entire time I was in the psych ward. For starters, we had violent women who acted aggressively, not just to me but to everyone else. After the psychotic woman tried to choke that poor girl, she was thankfully removed. Although she had been replaced with a crazed, wild-eyed Canadian woman who shouted all sorts of unsavoury stuff at the top of her voice. My heart was struggling with my blood pressure being up to the 170-180s. I now got twice-daily checks, but wasn't given any medication for it. A fat lot of good that did, but who was I to argue? It was painful having my BP checked so often. Every time they pumped up the armband to check my blood pressure, I felt this intense sensation shooting up my arm.

Keen to recover, I embraced all the therapies on offer. The next therapy was 'Pat the Dog Day'. I went along to the lounge room where the therapy dog, a golden Lab, like Monty would be brought in for us to pet. There were seats laid out in a row and I sat patiently waiting for my chance to pat the dog. I thought it would remind me of my sister's beautiful Lab. This dog smelt bad and only made me miss Monty even more. Monty never smelt and was well-groomed. He loved a shower, the warm water, being lovingly shampooed and blow-dried. I waited for my turn to stroke the dog and, after a few minutes I was off, the unwashed doggie smell was making me queasy.

Feeling low and teary, I didn't cry but had to cope and keep myself from danger. It wasn't safe to show any emotions. Otherwise,

I feared getting stuck in this place for longer or for life. The psych ward, with its prison doors, controlling staff, and bland hospital food in the grim canteen, was incredibly depressing. It was sad to see so many of the women looking in a right state and the defeated, broken-looking men with dead eyes. One chap, whom I had been introduced to by a woman on my ward, seemed nice enough but clearly manic.

Most people wanted to be alone, so I just observed them discreetly. Somehow I kept my spirits up. My strong spirituality and sense that I felt you never get what you can't handle in life helped me deal with this or whatever came my way. I remember so clearly feeling thrilled to be outside in nature. I even picked up some leaves and brought them back to my room. They made me feel alive in this negative, soul-crushing place, where it was impossible to sleep. Funny how on the night of my panic attack, the staff were nowhere to be seen. I quickly realised it was best to suffer in silence or find any vaguely empathetic member of staff. As I came off the drugs, I found that some staff were caring and endured a lot with agitated and unpredictable people and dealing with violent, infantile clashes.

The worst thing there, besides being drugged, was being terrified of the other inmates. With all the heightened emotions of people crying and drug-induced moods swings, things were kicking off all the time. I wasn't on drugs after I had my big panic attack and was surrounded by 19 people who were. Often some of the visitors coming in to see the other patients mistook me for a member of staff. I reassured them happily that I was 'sectioned'. I know, ludicrous, I would think to myself, a total injustice.

I did try to help people the best I could. One lady in her 60s was particularly lovely and confided that she was worried since she didn't know what the rules were. I told her that I didn't know them either. Apart from being locked up and the general schedule of eating and drug dispensing, it was all made up as they went along. I gave her a pad of paper and a pen and told her to write everything down. I watched other people's visitors come and go.

Thankfully I had Marcus and Sara to help me get through the bureaucracy of the place. Even though the head honcho took me off my meds, the staff still harassed me. One staffer said to me, "If you took your drugs, you would get out of here quicker", implying that it was my fault I was still here. What did she know about my life or experiences? Nothing. According to their shoddy records, I was bi-polar. I was getting hounded by them three times a day. Sometimes I found it hard to deal with it and rang Marcus, who would call to complain. Yet they told me Marcus had called asking why I wasn't taking my drugs. The place was doing my head in. They were understaffed and overwhelmed. It didn't help that the head psychiatrist had gone on holiday and hadn't left any notes about taking me off the medication. I was on a section, so they could do as they liked to me.

One thing I did do while locked up inside was to create a vision board, by cutting out images from magazines of my new life outside. I had picked up a John Lewis magazine and found a gorgeous-looking man sporting a beard. Well, the beard would have to go, I thought. Otherwise, he represented the new man I envisioned in my future life. I would do my design work and be creative and find some images to represent that too. My future was what I made it, so I was going to start from inside here.

Visioning is a powerful tool that I had used for years. It was a great way to put in pictures or words to create the life you wanted. I was taught to create a vision board by Ann Beazer, a friend I ended up working with. She had studied with Lucia Cappachione, the founder of the term 'Visioning©' Ann was such a wonderful soul who inspired many people and sadly died in 2021.

As they say in life, be careful what you wish for, it might actually come true. It was important for me to have hope for the future, and I needed something positive to live for.

That man that I imagined would turn up in my life suddenly, out of thin air—sooner than I thought possible.

17

Breakthrough: Sweet Release

The best day ever, I was finally going to be taken off the section. I had been told that morning that I had to go to a tribunal to appeal against my section. This would take place on the upcoming Monday. I was given a piece of paper with the names of solicitors on it. I had to choose one and call them to support me and put forward my case. That was my only way out of here. I rang Marcus and asked him which solicitor I should go for. He chose one and I wrote a long email outlining my situation. I was feeling stressed about it but knew my freedom depended on it. In the midst of writing the email, I heard a knock on my door. It was the man himself, the head psychiatrist, Dr Stephan, who asked if I would see a student psychologist. He explained that he would sit in on the session, but I had to pretend he wasn't in the room. More games, as if I hadn't had enough. I wanted to continue writing to the solicitor, but now another job thrust upon me.

The head psychiatrist took me to another room where the student was sitting. He was a young Asian guy who looked quite sweet. I was guided to sit in the seat opposite him, while the psychiatrist sat close by, pretending to ignore us. The student fired off a set of questions which I answered the best I could. Afterwards, Dr Stephan sent me back to my cell and said he'd come back for me in ten minutes. When he eventually returned, he took me to yet another room, the lounge this time, and asked me to take a seat opposite. He could see I was nervous and stressed. Then he dropped a bombshell and said he diagnosed me with acute stress reaction, also known as shock, mental shock or simply shock. He explained it was a psychological condition arising in response to a terrifying or traumatic event. I couldn't believe my luck, after all this time, finally someone was listening to me. The head psychiatrist had seen sense and realised I was recovering better without the drugs.

After explaining everything, he said, "I'm releasing you from your section, as of this moment."

"Wow, thank you," I said, letting it all sink in. Oh my God, another shock but I could have kissed him. "That's made my day, my week, my year."

And just like a flip of a lid, my world was upturned again. I was so happy and stunned. "Thank you again," I said, "And I'm so sorry if I've been rude when we had our earlier meeting. But I was so stressed about having a panic attack."

"Today's my last day too," he replied, his lips curling into a smile. "I'm taking a week off work."

"Are you going on holiday?" I asked.

"No, just a bit of DIY at home."

I laughed to myself, thinking, DIY, what a perfect hobby. He would have complete control over a piece of wood and some screws, whereas in this nuthouse he had to deal with a load of crazed and overemotional women and their unpredictable outbursts. The psychiatrist smiled, and he appeared happy I was on my way to being well again. We agreed, if I wanted, I could stay longer if I was scared of going outside on my own or if I needed to build up my confidence. I had been through hell, so small steps were needed.

Just as I stepped outside the psychiatrist's office, still in shock that I could actually leave, Kelly was waiting to take me out for my two-hour reprieve. She sat biting her nails, looking anxious.

"Good news," I said as soon as I caught her eye. "I've been released from my section, so I can leave now or whenever I like."

She looked disappointed and slightly pissed off. "You know,

Alice, it upset me so much that you've been locked up. I've been crying all the time while you've been in here," she said, and then added, "But you needed to go someplace safe and it wasn't all about you."

"You thought I needed to be shut away in a madhouse?" I said, stunned, as we stepped out into the street.

"Why couldn't you just be happy for me?"

"I am happy for you–"

"Really?" I cut her off, incensed, "I was the one sectioned.

Not you."

She had forgotten it was all her good work that contributed to me getting locked up in the first place. Being blocked by her husband in the street, the pair of them calling the police and an ambulance for me had all contributed to pushing me to the edge of insanity. Yet somehow she managed to make it all about her and her suffering.

"Kelly, I don't want to argue or talk about it." I was exhausted by this point and wanted to enjoy being outside and I was off my section at long last.

As we walked through the park, I took in all the beautiful trees, the birds, and the earthy scents and revelled in the feeling of freedom. I needed to connect with nature and feel alive again. We walked into town to the shopping centre. Southampton was not the most appealing place to be. So we went upstairs to the John Lewis café, my new home-from-home, for a coffee and cake.

The bright lights of the shopping mall were so enticing to a person who had spent two weeks in grim, grey prison-like confinement. Wandering around the beauty section of the store, we went to the Clarins counter. I wanted to buy some perfume so I could smell nice and feel good about myself. I wanted to wash away my marriage and the feelings I had shared with him. I wanted to cleanse myself from ever having a relationship with that dreadful man who had treated me so badly. I couldn't even think of him as an ex-husband since I barely knew him. Who was he anyway? I knew the other version of him, the kind one, the loving guy, not the one who woke me up with such devastating news and then pissed off to work without a care in the world. Surely this man wasn't right in the head?

We popped into the Apple store again since I was still having problems with my new iPad. The staff were helpful and kind and asked me to take a seat as they downloaded the new system onto the iPad. I could see Kelly was impatient and kept going outside to smoke. She seemed anxious and irritated by me and was constantly on her phone.

She bought me some stuff for my nails from a guy who had a stall inside the shopping mall. Since the downloading was taking ages, I told Kelly to go home and that I would make my way back on my own. She didn't trust me and felt responsible for me. I reminded her that I was off my section and that the head psychiatrist had released me so I could go wherever I pleased. I chatted with the Apple store chap who was lovely and showed me a photo of his new baby, and when we left he gave me a hug. I felt moved by the hug and nearly cried as no one had actually hugged me since I had been locked up. I hadn't felt this connection of human kindness for a while,.

When everything was sorted, Kelly and I were off in a taxi to make sure I got back in one piece, securely back into the hospital. It broke my heart that my friend of 45 years didn't even trust me now. She saw me as a "dangerous, unpredictable person". For the first time in ages, I was starting to feel kind of euphoric being able to go out like the others. I was not mad and I was now allowed to be a free person in the world. I was being given my life back in some small way and I felt truly grateful.

When I got back to the hospital, I realised I had forgotten to eat. We had been so busy sorting things out that I hadn't felt hungry. Now being back in the unit, the kitchen in the canteen was shut and no longer serving food. I spoke to one of the staff, who suggested I go outside and get something to eat. I didn't feel I could go outside alone. Southampton wasn't a nice place, particularly in this rougher part of town.

I ventured to my room, but the deranged Canadian in the room opposite was howling again. She made the staff jump so it wasn't just me. I called Sara to tell her I was off my section and she sounded thrilled. It was like being released from a prison sentence, which it certainly felt like for her and me. I knew she had felt helpless seeing her little sister suffering even more after what had been thrown at me. It was like a dream come true. Although we were taking it cautiously and I agreed to stay another week to adjust to the normal world.

The Canadian woman was in the throes of her nightly screaming and baying at the moon, so I locked myself in my cell for fear of what she would do next. I could call for help on my buzzer if necessary. Since I hadn't eaten anything all day, I thought I would try to buy some snacks from the vending machines. I didn't feel safe on my own yet, in this dodgy neighbourhood. When I nipped out of my room, the Canadian was shouting about lesbians. Off I went to the canteen, where I ran into Bill, a nice guy I had chatted to a few times before. He had been in here several times before and had a wife and children outside.

I felt safer in the canteen, safety in numbers I thought. I didn't think the Canadian would come out to the canteen so I could have some respite from the rude shouting and swearing that went on for hours. After the strangling incident, I wasn't taking any risks. I couldn't afford to be attacked by her, which would only set me back. Bill was sitting with another guy called Jamie. I told them I was off my section. They were delighted that I would restart my life very soon. Bill had some crisps and biscuits in his room and went and got them for me.

Jamie couldn't take his eyes off me. His eyes were beautiful sparkly blue, ones you don't forget in a hurry. Somewhere in his early-50s, he looked a little weathered but attractive with a warm smile that invited trust. Jamie asked what happened to me and told me about how awful his wife had been to him. He went into long-winded detail about how he lost his father and hadn't been told until six months after he died. Still, he seemed sane and kind.

When it got to 9 pm, we were asked to leave the canteen and Jamie said he hadn't finished telling me his story. He asked for my number and suggested that we could catch up tomorrow.

Since I was staying a week longer, I tried to make my cell a little more homely. I put all the photos and bits I had found in my bag on my pinboard. A sweet photo of my nephew Sam, alongside snaps of other nieces and nephews when they were small. I had decorated my room with a nice postcard of a sunset and put the dried leaves I had collected from the park on the windowsill that overlooked the tarmacked smoking area. I wanted to feel a connection to nature, however tenuous. I had found a letter from Stephanie and Marcus, which kept me going when I felt I was never getting out of here. I stuck it on the pinboard.

Dear Alice,

Stephanie and I are so proud of you, for the amazing eloquent way you are dealing with your immense grief, brought upon you by others. We are certain in time that you will emerge as the 'Wahe Guru' victor as your journey for justice gathers momentum, day by day, week by week, you will get stronger. You may have temporary setbacks, but you will emerge and there will be no stopping you. And we will be there for you, all the way, for as long as it takes. You are precious to us all, an intelligent articulate, beautiful, loving person worthy of the very best (or just adequate!) happy and healthy life.

Hopefully, your Dorset experience, together with your 'special' family around you, will make you extremely strong and empower you for your future happiness. Your dear dad was an inspiration to all of us, his love, bravery and devotion to all who touched him, and he will guide you through this turbulent storm.

Please take plenty of rest... sleep well and remember we will always be there for you.

Love Marcus and Stephanie xx

Those words touched my heart and gave me great strength and a glint of hope I could recover from this and that at least two people believed in me. I was still someone worthy of a life and this was a reminder to ask my dad, in spirit, to guide me on my path. He would be there for me, even though I felt alone. I had to keep the faith.

Reading that letter again, I was touched to tears as they encapsulated such kindness, foresight, and life-saving words for me. I would keep reading the words, the words were real, had solidity and told me a story of the future life I would live. I could do it; I could make it through. The words told me I was loved, even though I felt nothing, besides the pain of my loss.

Other items I found in there were pictures of me as a child. A photo of me in fancy dress at the Silver Jubilee Street party we had back in 1977. I was 10 years old and dressed as a royal scrapbook and had gone in for the fancy-dress competition. I came in second place or first I can't remember. I recalled how awkward it was to walk in between the two large pieces of cardboard, my body literally sandwiched together. It was topped off with a homemade bowler hat with a Union Jack on it. I was standing beside my cousin, who looked unhappy and was holding a tiny Union Jack flag, in the hallway of my old house. I recognised the spiral-patterned carpet popular back then. I was wearing my first pair of jeans, not dark denim but a turquoise colour my sister had bought for me and my favourite top, a turquoise flannel hoodie. I was smiling in the photo, but looked a little awkward in the restrictive cardboard outfit. That photo ended up in the local newspaper.

Inside the envelope, I found a cute black-and-white snap of me as a chubby-cheeked baby, sitting on the kitchen worktop. My Pinky and Perky mug, of two piglets dressed up in clothes sitting on the shelf behind me. My chubby hands were clasping an empty bowl. There was one of me as a teenager, looking happy in a white lace-edged top. Laura had added the lace as it was fashionable in the 80s. There was one of Dad when he was building our laundry room, with one arm up against the wall, looking straight into the camera with a big smile.

The next photo reminded me of recent happier times, when Mum had her 80th birthday, we threw a party for her at the house. She looked happy being back in our family home. As I flicked through, I found the first photo I had taken of Monty, the adorable adopted golden Lab. He looked quite small and skinny, and you could see his ribs showing. There was another shot of Monty, the first time I met him, lying alongside me on my mother's swing. He was a special gift to our family, a uniting force to one and all. On the back of the envelope, TRUST ME was written in big capital letters. I needed to remind myself and others to trust me. I had lost trust in practically everything.

It was amazing what I had gathered in my electric-blue coloured handbag, I had bought it so I could sling it across my shoulder when we are going to have the children. I had subconsciously gathered a world of photos to remind me of my life in my darkest hour, yet not knowing I was going to be locked up, just knowing I was on a journey somewhere.

My confidence had taken a battering being abandoned, discarded by my ex and shut away in a mental ward, but I was strong enough to get through this. I felt sorry for the other women here—nice, intelligent people who didn't love themselves. Nor did I, really, so we had that much in common. And while I constantly felt scared, I realised everyone in here was in pain, I forgot about myself and wanted to help others. My focus was surviving amid the madness and threats of intimidation by staying in my room to write. This was teaching me something—not to take my freedom for granted and what I had in the outside world.

I had to make my environment a positive place with reminders of my other life. I envisioned my way out of here. Not thinking where about I would go when I got out. My sister Laura hadn't visited me, which was upsetting. When I told Marcus, he got Laura to send me a text, along with a lovely photo of Monty, saying she loved me. I knew she did deep down, but she couldn't deal with me. Since she lived with Mum, I felt betrayed by them both, yet still felt I had to apologise to them.

The next day, I saw the lovely Dr Misra. I wanted to talk to him. He wanted to do an ECG to check my heart. I had spoken to Dr Misra before about the children and the number of my room. He asked me my date of birth and told me I was a 'one' and that Isabella was a 'one'. He said ones were leaders who could handle a lot in life. He said the number four meant overcoming obstacles. He had a spiritual side and suggested a few books to read about Sufism, a mystic religious practice mainly found in Islamic countries. Dr Misra thought that I should see an energy healer to help me. He confided that he had a spiritual guru, which I was keen to see too, whatever the religion, but sadly his guru was in Pakistan. We laughed about it, that it was a little too far for me to go. Finally, I had found someone who understood me, and Dr Misra shined a light on my circumstances. Slowly and steadily, things were improving.

Before coming into the unit, I felt some spiritual experiences. It was as if I had walked into another dimension. I had started the year before doing Kundalini yoga, a spiritual kind of yoga, made up of Kriya's and chanting mantras. I was reassured by my teacher that I wouldn't suffer from mental health problems if I practised, as it balances the physical and emotional self. Well, that was a joke on me, considering where I had ended up.

What I had been through was deep sudden grief for the loss of my children. I needed to know how I was going to cope with this. Singing my mantras had given me the strength to continue and liberated me from the inertia of depression. I still had a longing for reconciliation with my children. I had not wanted to give up, so I rambled on and on about what had happened to me. Dr Misra listened as he recognised the spiritual element in my situation. I told him 04.04 was my wedding day and now I was staying in a room with 04.04. This couldn't be a coincidence.

He gave me his time and spiritual knowledge, which helped me feel like he understood me. After losing trust in everyone, somehow I trusted him, surely this person was going to help me heal.

18

Falling into Another Trap

When one door closes, another door opens may be a terrible cliché, but it suddenly made sense. Jamie, the good-looking guy I had met in the canteen the other night, had started texting and saying how much he understood my situation. The intensity of his interest in me was flattering. He sent me kind texts saying that he wanted to be friends. He had those twinkly blue eyes. When I asked him why he was here, he recounted how he was picked by the police. They thought he was suicidal, but he said it was just a cry for help. He had just found out his father had died six months previously. His family had not bothered to call him about it. It came as a massive shock and he had got drunk and sat on a bridge in Southampton. They had brought him in on a voluntary basis. He was freaked out about being here among these other people who were drugged up. One guy in his ward had been in there for over two years.

Jamie started texting constantly, saying lovely, supportive things. He seemed so caring and sweet and told me—wait for it—that my husband was the biggest loser as he had lost me and would one day regret what he had done. We met in the canteen and had lunch and later, dinner together. I had written the day I met him that 'I really liked him'. Unlike the other patients, he looked 'normal', and I could actually have a conversation with him. I had found a like-minded friend and it was exciting and new. We could relate to each other's circumstances. Secretly he looked a bit like the guy I had put in my vision board, the gorgeous man with the beard.

I couldn't begin to imagine what the future held for me. One thing was certain, I wanted a divorce. I needed protection from this man that had wrecked my life. A solicitor had been suggested in Surrey and Sara and Marcus took me to the meeting. A solicitor won't see you unless you were off your section. Thankfully, I had been released and I was leaving in a few days.

We met the young woman who was going to represent me, and we all sat around a large table. She asked me questions and took a few notes and the factual details. Solicitors don't care about emotions, they just put the clock on and proceed.

It was all a blur. I was starting to panic, but I was composed enough and said what needed to be done. The money was handed over and Marcus took me back to the unit. At least it was in motion and I would be divorced from this spineless liar, whom I felt was a threat to me, not physically but mentally and emotionally. My marriage had been a lie and I felt deeply violated by this man whom I thought had loved me, but was a virtual stranger to me now. After five years he hadn't given me the dignity to talk or even apologise for the mess he wrought. The main thing now was that I was taking control and Marcus and Sara were helping me get through this ordeal.

My new life off the section meant I could go into town, have a coffee and slowly transition back into the real world. I could get my emails and start contacting a few friends that may come and visit. My phone, was still the cheap red Nokia Sara had bought for me, a pay-as-you-go tariff, costing a bomb and I was continually running out of credit. Sara and Marcus weren't sure whether I should have my phone back yet, but it would be cheaper. I didn't want to be the bringer of bad news, but I needed visitors and some kind of connection.

I loved seeing the trees and being free again, but it was a little scary since I wasn't used to spending so much time outside. This was underlined by a heavy sadness that my life had fallen apart and there had been another miscarriage of justice. Why I had to suffer the indignity of being locked up on top of the heartbreak? All I knew was that I had to start reclaiming my place in the real world. One day I was sitting in a café, and I got an email from Marcus, saying he had looked into the adoption criteria and there was no way I was ever going to have the children on my own. I suddenly felt devastated, like my heart was breaking all over again. There would be nothing left of me. I thought that if I had survived this situation, then maybe they would let me adopt them on my own. I had even emailed the head of Andy's school and asked if he would write an email about all the extra work my husband had done and that this had caused him severe stress and to back out last minute. I needed evidence so I could go ahead and have the children as a single parent.

It was the same day that Jamie had promised to meet me for coffee in town but he was having trouble getting out of the building. I told him what had happened and he managed to get out for an hour with a chaperone. They wielded a lot of power in the psych ward, in a kind of self-important way. Jamie turned up with a support worker, who was quite creepy and gave me bad vibes. I gave Jamie some money to buy himself and the support worker coffee. Technically the psych ward staff weren't allowed to take anything off a patient, even a coffee, but he did and sat there watching us.

That email had been another crushing blow. I may have been off my section but the realisation that there was no way I would be able to adopt seemed like another knock. With all the stress and drugging, my memory must have gone. I had already emptied the house of children's things so it should have dawned on me there would be no adoption of the children ever. I just couldn't face the heartbreak of losing my life with them.

Jamie was supportive and his response allowed me to trust him at this crucial time, feeling a deep emptiness in my heart. We chatted for half an hour and then his chaperone, who was looking at his clock, whisked him away. We agreed to meet later in the canteen. Sitting alone in Café Nero, another new lounge room for my in-between life, in-between two worlds. I called Sara to tell her, she told me to keep my spirits up. I felt alone in a big world, with everyone playing a part except for me. I didn't have a life. I had my divorce and nothing else. I had half a house, which would soon be snatched away from me too. I had no one else to talk to. I would've called my mother but didn't want to worry her.

My uncle had been diagnosed with schizophrenia back in the 70s. We had spent our childhood living in fear of him coming around to our house. As we never knew if he was going to behave—dangerous or not, that is. He looked a bit like Elvis with thick black hair and a quiff. He was a big guy, so you wouldn't want to mess with him. My sisters and I were often told to go to our bedrooms and lock the door until he was gone. I can remember telling my school friends my uncle had schizophrenia, unaware of what it really meant. He wasn't a violent man but had had some unpredictable outbursts, so my parents were never sure how he would be, and my older siblings were scared of him. He would sometimes not take his meds and become violent during these times. I could remember feeling afraid of him and being told he had been stabbed while living in a mental hospital. So I was well aware that while in the psychiatric hospital, I had to keep myself safe. I had already been confronted by an aggressive woman and seen first-hand violence against another patient.

19

The Great Escape: November 1st 2014

Writing and mapping out my future plans inside was a way of conquering time and finding solace. Now that I was allowed to leave, the creeping anxiety of going out alone seemed overwhelming. One day Jamie suggested we go for an evening out. I wanted to go to the cinema and catch a film. First, he wanted to eat so we went to an Indian restaurant he knew. I felt nervous and a bit odd in my new life. We chatted away and I enjoyed just being out doing normal things. At the end of the meal, Jamie hadn't managed to get any money from his bank. He asked if I could pick up the bill and he would pay me back once he sorted out his Barclays account. I paid and by the time the meal was over it was too late for the cinema. So, since neither of us knew the area, we went to a bar nearby. Jamie was charming, chatty and kind. I felt almost normal being out and about, and relaxed finally.

Later, when it was time to head back, Jamie confided that he rang the unit, pretending to be my brother Tom, and told them that I was out for the night. I was stunned and had no idea why he would do this. I'd had a few drinks and needed to go back to my room, where I felt safe. Now I couldn't go back there. Jamie suggested we find a hotel. I went along with it, even though I was scared. We got a hotel room for the night. What happened next, he seduced me. The next morning, I relaxed enjoying the luxury of a hot bath instead of a shower, I began to feel like a normal person again. Since, once again, he didn't have any money. I paid the bill, although he assured me, he was going to pay me back. We returned separately back to the hospital.

Now that I wasn't on a section, I was free to leave whenever I wanted. Jamie wanted to leave the clinic on the same day as me. The plan was to go home with Jamie and get my car so that I would have it when I was ready to be discharged. We caught the train and a taxi to my house, which felt strange since it had been unlived in for over a month. We drove back to Southampton, and I parked the car ready for the final escape on the coming Friday. I was looking forward to leaving the unit.

To enable a patient to leave the hospital you have to have one night away. As I had had one night stay in the hotel I didn't need another one, so I was technically allowed to leave the unit. As usual, I didn't really understand the rules. It was a bit like Chinese whispers. The next day when I came back from a visit the city centre, I got one of the support workers, a lovely Irish chap, to open my door. I found my room was stripped bare of all my things. I stood there horrified and distressed. All the parts of the little life I had created to support me in my sudden change had been removed. I no longer existed. I tried to hold back the tears of hurt and humiliation that I had been pushed out in such a harsh, inhumane way.

I rushed over to the staff area and saw the same woman, who knew my room had been cleared and, instead of telling me, allowed me to go back to see it was empty.

Feeling slightly confused and composing myself, I asked her politely, "Where are all my things?"

"The room has been packed up. We're a hospital, and we needed the bed."

My impulse was to tell her that this was a bloody psych ward and how could they treat people so harshly. Instead, I swallowed my anger and said quietly, "Aren't I a human being?"

She glared at me. "Well, now you can get on with your life."

Get on with my life... How the hell do I do that?

No apology, nothing. She had no idea, how I was feeling about the fact they had gone into my private space and rummaged through my things and packed them away like I was a dead person. She said something to the nice Irish chap, who took me to the front desk, where he extracted the two large brown paper bags and left them in the reception area.

Turning away, my eyes glistening with tears, I walked slowly over to my car in shock. Then I thought I need to stand up for myself to be seen as a human being and I went back to the reception.

"Can you please carry the bags to my car, so I can sort them out?" I asked the Irish guy calmly. "I want to leave some clothes for people who, like me, don't have any when they come here."

"Sure." He picked up my bags and carried them to my car. Handing him a pile of donated clothes, he took them and wished me well.

And just like that, it was over. I didn't come out fixed or feeling any better, as Laura and Kelly expected I would. If anything, at that moment, I felt really sad and humiliated— again feeling rejected, and cast away. The horrors of that day, 30 September 2014, were still having lasting repercussions. I seemed to be cursed. When would things ever improve for me?

I drove my Mini around the corner and Jamie was standing there with his one bag. He got into the car and I barely had time to process what happened. I wasn't even sure where I was going. Somewhere far away from this shit hole of a city and far away from the terrible hospital. I had to put all the pain behind me. I needed to escape.

Jamie suggested Lymington, a riverside village in the beautiful New Forest. We found a fantastic B&B called Bosun's Chair, a former Georgian coach house with a pub and rooms, and decided to stay for the night. The three-storey inn had a rambling garden and bar-restaurant, where Jimi Hendrix jammed in 1970, before the Isle of Wight Festival, three weeks before his death.

I was in a dream world. I felt safe in those elegant rooms and pretty village, with wild ponies and sweet-faced donkeys roaming everywhere, and Jamie listened to me. I was exhausted, and Jamie was too. We needed a bit of a holiday from everything. I couldn't face going back home and still felt threatened by Andy and the thought of seeing him again. I was living under a permanent black cloud of anxiety and gloom.

The next day Jamie had his own issues to deal with, so I was involved in his stuff. He took me to a series of graves, including his father's, in the New Forest. We went and put some flowers on it. Again, he gave me the sob story about how he wasn't told his father had died and how hurt he was that his family didn't talk to him. He was especially angry at his stepmother who was contesting his father's will. I genuinely wanted to help him and was living in a surreal world of visiting grave after grave, this aunt and that uncle. He enjoyed tidying up their gravestones. I chose some nice flowers, this time yellow roses for peace. We took photos for him to send to his very old aunt and uncle in Jersey where they still lived.

I could relate since I had lost my father and still felt his loss deeply, in addition to the sorrow of losing my adoptive children. I would often find myself crying when I woke up each morning. My heartache isolated me further. I felt like I was wading through quicksand on a daily basis and constantly going under. Now that I was out of the psych ward, I needed support but couldn't rely on my family. Jamie promised to look after me and support me through the mud pool of life. I thought he was a gift from the universe to help me through all the suffering I had endured those last few weeks

Jamie and I had seemed to get on well. He liked travelling as much as I did. He wanted to go back and live in Sweden, and we dreamed of going on holiday together when this waiting game was over. He was easygoing and liked the food I cooked. Above all, he supported me in my emotional trauma. After a few days of milling around the New Forest, I returned home with Jamie.

We couldn't live in B&B's forever. It was not only expensive but I had limited access to funds since the bank closed my account. Andy stole all our savings, and put them into another account in his name. I trusted Jamie would pay me back, like he constantly promised. Why wouldn't I trust him? I had trusted my husband and look where that had got me. But I had to trust someone or no one.

20

High Water Everywhere

Feeling lost and restless, I wasn't sure what to do next or where to go. I knew I didn't feel comfortable going back to my house and now I had another person hanging on me. Jamie and I had known each other for barely a week, which in itself should've been worrying. With my high blood pressure and constant anxiety attacks, a family friend agreed to let us stay in their lovely holiday home in Selsey, a peaceful seaside town in West Sussex, full of rolling cliffs and twisty lanes.

In addition to the sadness and sudden loss of my former life, I had to deal with the trauma of having been shunted into a psych ward and not given any kindness in my recovery. I had been left to work it out myself. I knew Marcus and Sara would support me as much as they could, but I still had to deal with all the shit that had suddenly landed at my door. My confidence was shattered, my spirit broken and I was scared of my own shadow. I wasn't talking to Laura and was unable to face my mother yet. All my friends were busy with their jobs and had their lives in London.

I had to keep on acting and make up a new life somehow. The truth is I didn't feel fully safe with Jamie, who was a complete stranger, and I didn't want him to move into my house with me. He was quite needy and a huge distraction, and I had enough awfulness to deal with.

I met my brother Tom's friends, Jackie and Karen, at the caravan site, right by a beautiful sandy coastline near Witterings. It was a cosy and gorgeously decorated caravan with all the mod cons. Over coffee, I told Jackie and Karen about everything that happened over the last couple of months and they were visibly upset by the situation and my shaky appearance. I started having a coughing fit halfway through our conversation and Jamie just looked at me. It was while staying here that I had the realisation of what on earth was going on in my life. I would often wake up crying into my pillow. The days were spent in a daze running around here and there, back and forth to my house. Between my anxiety and soaring blood pressure, I was exhausted and drained. Jamie still didn't have any access to money, which added more pressure. I already had too much to worry about. I couldn't do much, making meals, driving and lying down a lot, which meant I often fell asleep. I was a shadow of my former self, a ghost without emotions. I was constantly distracted by Jamie's needs; he needed a letter written or this or that; constant trips to his bank. As usual, I had trouble sleeping and would wake up very early. Trying to stay calm, I continued to journal secretly to try and unravel my emotions and figure out my next move.

In London, where I had lived for over 25 years, I had most of my network of friends who either had hectic full-time jobs or families, so I couldn't bother them. It made me realise in the last seven years I had spent down here, I hadn't made many new friends.

I wasn't good at asking for help and Jamie just seemed to slip into my life without me noticing. He was prepared to care for me, but I had to sub him money daily for his cigarettes and living expenses. I thought I loved Jamie, but I didn't know if he actually loved me. We had found each other in our hour of need and were helping each other along. He believed that I was okay and he was too. No one from my family was calling me to see if I needed help, aside from Sara, my closest sibling, who called regularly and was convinced I was doing fine.

I felt threatened by Andy. But how could he still get to me and hurt me after all the damage he had done already? There was the constant threat of him coming around to the house, needing a book for school, or this or that. I had reams of emails from my solicitor and a bill to match all the things he needed. Conveniently for him, he didn't get a solicitor, but just used mine, seeking their advice and ramping up my expenses. My solicitor also told him his rights, leaving me in an even more vulnerable position. I was living in a whirlpool, trying to manage, day by day, and Jamie needed me too. He had no one and nowhere to go. I had an empty house and needed the company of another person since I couldn't cope with the dark nights and life generally. I convinced myself that the universe had found this man for me. I was starting to fall for him. It turned out we had similar life experiences of getting out of a troubled marriage and lots of shared interests, which felt promising. He did yoga with me, was happy to see a healer and agreed to receive a blessing from Mother Meera. So he must be okay, mustn't he?

I had something to hold onto and make this new life worth living. With the grief of losing the children looming over me, I felt dead inside. The treatment I had received from my husband had been a massive blow to my self-worth. I needed someone by my side and Jamie fulfilled this need. He turned vegetarian since I didn't eat meat—although I sometimes ate fish and was a pescatarian. He also stopped drinking coke, although he liked his cigarettes. I couldn't stand his smoking and it was expensive, a cost I could do without. He kept reassuring me that he would pay me back. I had enough problems so I was happy to go along with it. I was alone otherwise, and he would be going soon once his job started. He had a heart problem, too, which would arise now and again.

I could feel myself hanging by a very thin thread. I was trying to rebuild my life, but was also leading a parallel life with a stranger. How had I imagined or manifested this person, just so I wouldn't have to be alone? Like an imaginery friend. The pain of what had happened felt like it had taken away my whole life, which in effect it had—my husband, my future life with children, my security, my home, my freedom, my family, my friends, my personal safety.

Somehow I was determined to get through this. But equally, I was exhausted and now had a divorce to sort out. Andy wanted access to the house. In the meantime, Jamie apparently had a few problems where he had been staying with a friend and, after this episode, he couldn't go back, so he was stuck without a place to live. It was only a temporary solution I kept telling myself and he would soon have his money and move to Dorset. Dorset just happened to be the place that I wanted to move to, yet another thing we had in common. Days melted into weeks. What had been a temporary situation became permanent. I didn't feel safe living alone and, if nothing else, having Jamie around was reassuring. He created some level of protection. I needed to rest, sleep and come to terms with my strange new existence.

Barely out of the clinic, alongside dealing with the divorce, I needed to face the adoption agency alone. I had championed the agency all along, telling people over the two-year process how supportive and great they were, but when it all fell through they were nowhere to be found. I was under the illusion that someone would be despatched to my house to offer some support. Our social worker told me my husband was a "fantasist and I was to destroy everything". She hadn't thought about me, or my feelings, only telling me she knew I would be in no state to have the children or recover in time to adopt them.

Jamie drove me to Reading for the meeting to take back the children's belongings to the agency. We had been given some toys their birth parents had bought them. They weren't anything much, but they might miss them, so they needed to be returned just for the record. Thankfully, months previously I had met Lia, a lovely lady who had adopted a child, and I asked her to support me in this meeting.

I saw the interim assistant director of the agency and all sat down in the room. The building was familiar we had attended a variety of workshops there. I noticed it had recently been decorated and didn't look quite so dismal as I had recalled. The director sat opposite, with Lia to my left side. We discussed the situation and I asked about some support, and he said outright "there wasn't any". Although he did say I was still "officially an adopter", but I would need to be reassessed again in April 2015, that was if I was to go through the adoption process again alone. He was sympathetic, but there was nothing he could do. The council that the children were coming from had cut off all contact with the agency on the day the adoption had fallen through, so he didn't know what happened to the children. Lia advised me not to say anything negative about my social worker, and to keep the meeting professional in case I wanted to adopt in the future.

The interim director asked me to write a letter to the children explaining why I hadn't been able to adopt them. I wrote a letter over the next few days and sent it to him. It was a challenge and brought back a flood of emotions. I eventually emailed it to him. He replied abruptly and said that this was not the kind of letter he required after all. All my time spent writing it had been emotional and difficult for me, but it was not what was best for the children, so I agreed to his letter. He could've saved me a lot of emotion by telling me in the beginning what I was allowed to say to them.

15 November 2014

Dear Isabella and Alfie,

It was one of the happiest days in my life when my husband Andy and I were contacted to see if we would like to adopt you and become your mum and dad. When we saw your photos and talked with people who know you well, we felt it would be fantastic to become your parents. Sadly, just as we were about to meet you for the first time, Andy and I found that we had some unhappiness in our own life, which we would have to spend a lot of time to sort out. This meant it was not the right time for us to become mum and dad to two wonderful children who need a new family to grow up with and where they can be very happy. I am sure that there are many families who would love to adopt you and will be able to give you the love and happiness that you need, and I know that people will make sure they find the right family for you.

I will always remember you and send you my very best wishes for a happy life.

With Love,

Alice

I was heartbroken all over again. Isabella and Alfie would remain in my thoughts, even though I would never meet them or see them grow up. I knew that I would always have a special place in my heart for them. That was all I was allowed and I would take that. I would never have children of my own or experience the ups and downs of motherhood. In the future, I knew I would have to dig deep to recover, create and adapt to a new kind of life, one worth living. At this point, I was still in survival mode. I'd always joked while going through the adoption that if it all fell through, I would get a dog. I loved my sister's dog Monty who had given me so much love and joy as animals do. That was the only thing I could think of that would fill my need to nurture something, the pure, whole-hearted love of a dog.

Soon I was back in my old home and Jamie came too. He was homeless and, although not penniless. He told me he was getting money into his account from renting a house with his ex-wife and didn't know where she lived or if he was getting a divorce. Still, we made plans for the future. Funnily enough, we wanted the same things out of life, a house in Dorset, and a dog—well he wanted two dogs. On paper, we seemed to be a perfect match. How lucky I was to have found him. I had slipped out of one world into another.

Weeks turned into months, and nothing seemed to move along or get resolved. I was not in my right mind, but life had to go on.

Since I felt threatened and bullied by my ex-husband and didn't know how to cope with him and the solicitors, I would visit the odd friend now and again just for a bit of respite.

21

Winter Wonderland

Some good news, Jamie was taking me to Sweden for Christmas. We finally had something to look forward to. I needed a change of scenery and a rest from this transitional life. His ex-partner and two grown-up children lived in Sweden, and they had invited us to stay in their holiday home. His daughter Kristina was a house model for a Danish clothing company and his son Christophe worked in the oil industry. Jamie had it all sorted and we would stay at his son's house and spend Christmas day with his ex-partner and her family. He adored his ex-wife, and she had a new partner called Sven. I was determined to learn some Swedish before going, so I got a book and started with a few verbs. Jamie claimed he could speak Swedish but was a bit rusty. Also, at this time, his boss, Mark, had said he could live rent-free in an empty house in Canford Cliffs in Dorset while he waited for house prices to go up and that would be around January. At long last, things seemed to be working out.

Well, that fantasy shattered at the airport.

There was only one problem regarding Jamie's passport—he only had a Swedish one, his UK passport had expired and he hadn't replaced it yet. His daughter was going to send it over. For any sensible person, this should've been a huge red flag. Why was his passport in Sweden and why couldn't he just go to the embassy in London to get another one? As it turned out later he had no proof of ID, so unable to get a new passport.

Jamie gave some weird, detailed story about how his daughter had gotten angry with him and ripped up his passport. He had managed to get a new one and Kristina was bringing it over to London. All we had to do was meet up with her. She was going to come and stay with us. Well, that was the plan. I had seen photos of Kristina, she was a stunning blonde and apparently very high-maintenance. He told me she didn't catch trains and wanted him to meet her at the airport and take her to London. Of course, he needed to borrow my car, though he was embarrassed about driving my Mini since his daughter was used to being driven in an Audi or something of that calibre. He would have to slum it in my Mini, but it needed a clean first.

On the day his daughter was due to come, she texted saying she developed a cold, but that she was looking forward to meeting me. She had texted her father and apologised and so we decided to go up and collect the passport. We drove up at the weekend and went to Covent Garden and had lunch. We were to meet her later in the day, but she didn't turn up. She had apparently left her bag in a cloakroom at a club the previous night with his passport in it. We went to a pub and waited for the club to open and then she could give him his passport. She was to meet us later. I was exhausted by now, and Jamie said let's have dinner and she can pay for it. I was furious but had to keep calm.

His daughter sounded like a nightmare, a real diva, but this was taking it too far. He later told me she had gotten drunk and caught for drunken driving. I was busy trying to cope with my divorce, doing some freelance work and now managing all his ceaseless needs. All the while the money he was borrowing was going up and up. I looked forward to being paid back and moving into a real relationship, with him having a job etc.

It was lucky his ex-partner worked for an airline so at least we could get free flights to Stockholm, but he didn't have his passport yet. There was always some obstacle or two in the way. He still hadn't paid me the money I had advanced him for the jobs he was doing. Nothing seemed to go right for him or us. It was never-ending. It was all beyond my control so I tried to be patient. Surely, eventually, it would come together. I just needed a holiday and Scandinavia really interested me, so I focused on the positive.

I had a suspicion his daughter wasn't coming—of course, she wasn't. So it was arranged we would meet her at the airport and all fly to Stockholm together. When we got to the airport, she had flown back on an earlier flight but had given Jamie's passport to Susanna, a friend of hers who was going to meet us at the airport. It was still going to happen. Next problem Susanna had got the tube all the way to the airport and her phone had died and she couldn't find us, so she had gone back to London. She would meet us at the pub later. This time her boyfriend would bring her but again, we waited all night, and they never came. This happened for days, so we spent two nights in one hotel and two nights in another in London. All the days were spent at Heathrow Terminal 5, sitting around, seething and drinking coffee. The big wait. Jaw-droppingly unbelievable.

He had a way of spinning stories, that blossomed like weeds beneath the intricately woven lies. It was hard to keep up and think straight. Looking back, I should have seen it coming, as we waited and waited, and nothing ever happened. My scepticism about him deepened. Despite the madness of this, I still kind of trusted him. Clearly, I was insane and in denial. Perhaps it was the desperation of my own broken-down situation. I had no one else and I didn't want to celebrate Christmas since I had nothing to celebrate—no family, no friends, and nothing to look forward to.

Fed up and furious, I rang my healer friend, Linda, who advised me to go home. Otherwise, I could be waiting at the airport for a long time, since the passport was never coming. His daughter had let him down. Her friend had let him down. Obviously, he said it wasn't his fault. The excitement of going on holiday was gone. If only I had realised then what a compulsive liar he was. He was so convincing and I got sucked in. When I think back to all the lies he told me it was humiliating that I was so gullible. For anyone in their right mind, it was glaringly obvious that he was a scammer and his stories were incredulous. I must have been very forgiving or very stupid to have fallen for his web of lies.

At that point, I still believed he was going off to work—as a property surveyor, of all things, someone who was homeless and penniless—and I had to provide him with a car and cash to do the job. His boss just never paid him, he'd say, it was so unfair and so stressful. The house was the next thing. We would drive down to Dorset and his friends wouldn't meet him to give him the keys or the money that was owed to him. Another time, he was going to Dorset to get the keys, and I went along. When he said that his friend wasn't coming with the keys, I went ballistic on Branksome Chine Beach. I'd finally had enough. He just argued back and, of course, blamed everything constantly going wrong on someone else or his bad luck. This was slowly killing me. He was like a vampire draining me of every ounce of energy.

Then, Jamie told me that his friend Mark was selling the house and he could have a flat nearby to live in. Such a huge relief. Jamie had all his stuff in a container which Mark had arranged to be delivered down from Surrey to Dorset. I had even paid for a removal company to do it for him just to get rid of him.

The debts on my cards were mounting up and Barclays, his so-called bank, hadn't come through; the inheritance money from his father's will hadn't come through; the work he had done for Mark hadn't come through. I started to panic, who would believe me that this man was living in my house and taking money from me? Well, I was complicit. He wasn't holding a gun to my head, I was a willing giver. He knew all along I was broke but continued scrounging off me. Surely he couldn't be such a heartless liar, could he? I would search my mind and search for clues. How could I, a generous and caring person, attract another devious man, who, like my ex-husband, was just ripping me off.?

Other things unsettled me. Like Andy, Jamie was very secretive around his phone. His little hands constantly gripped his phone and he was constantly deleting texts. I put this out of my mind.

I started writing in a diary. There was I making him meals, buying him cigarettes and wine, taking him out for meals, and hiring him a car. Oh my God, I must be mental. No wonder I was locked up. Alone and isolated, I started to feel trapped about what could I do. Tell my family? He knew where I lived. I had lent him my iPad, although he had said he left it at work. I kept on making deadlines. If the money was paid back by next week somehow, I would try and get rid of him. But how?

There were so many ways the money was coming to me. Sven, his ex-partner's new husband, would pay my card off. He was going to put the money into my account from Sweden. The entire time I hoped it would happen. I was so stressed my hair was starting to fall out and shedding all over the house, like a moulting cat's winter coat. Sensing I was going to have another breakdown if I didn't do something, I hatched a plan to escape from him for good. My niece's wedding was coming up and I would go and stay at my sister's house. I was now waking up daily crying and feeling sick to my stomach. I was angry with myself. How could I get stuck in such a trap again? Another lying, parasitic bastard in my life. I had fallen down a black hole, suffocating and scrambling to get out.

The last week Jamie had gone back every day to the bank. I had moved into my spare room as I could no longer bear him near me. I knew very clearly this man who had seemed nice, started to look uglier and uglier. I had to do some acting and plan my escape. There was no way I could ask for help, who would help me now out of this self-perpetuated mess?

Jamie took the train to Bournemouth and, again, no money. He called me saying he needed a room to stay the night. He was lost and had no money. I booked him into a hotel again. How many more times was I going to book him into a hotel? I wanted to catch him out, so I drove down to Bournemouth. Again nothing happened. We stayed in a hotel for two nights while we waited for his boss Mark. He had come up with yet another plan. His son Christophe was flying over with his girlfriend with the cash and would pay it into my account. I paid for yet another hotel room. His son would pay the money, apparently, and I would be at my niece's wedding far away from him.

I gave him some cash and drove off, badly shaken, hoping to never see him again. It was like I was on some bad TV drama escaping another lying bastard, who again was only interested in my money. Not that I had any. My ex was refusing me money from my own savings while this arsehole was racking up my credit cards. If it wasn't bad enough, my solicitor was making money off me left, right and centre.

Before leaving, we sat in a hotel reception and I gave Jamie a book called Calm and told him to get some help. I gave him the details to pay off my accounts. I knew at that moment, I never wanted to see Jamie again. I was up to my eyeballs in debt, but that had to be better than living with another shameless, lying, money-grubbing arsehole.

I came away feeling not only incredibly sad, and humiliated, but also fearful of what he would do next. I drove and drove wishing in every moment to put him behind me, but knowing I had an avalanche of debts because of him. I went straight home and packed my bags for the wedding.

I met Sara in a little café in Ripely and she immediately knew something was wrong. I burst out crying, telling her how I'd lent a "thieving stranger a ridiculous amount of money."

"Oh my God," my sister moaned she could hardly believe what I was telling her.

"And now I'm trying to get rid of him. I seem to be afflicted by him."

"We have to call the police." She was trying to get her head around the crazy idea that I was giving money to a man I met in the pysch ward. We had some last-minute preparations for the wedding. While we were running around the shops, he called and wanted some money for yet another hotel room since his son had been delayed. He kept on calling and texting that he was cold and had nowhere to sleep. Sara told me I had to ignore him, but he kept leaving messages.

Later I told Sara and her husband Dan the whole excruciatingly painful story, as improbable and crazy as it sounded, they understood and advised me to get protection and go to the police.

The next day was the wedding day, so I kept my phone switched off. The wedding was beautiful, and I felt happy being surrounded by my family. I also felt sad that my own marriage was over, but here was my niece starting her life as a married woman. I acted my way through the day and had some wine to pull me through.

I had made it. I was now away from that person. Who was he anyway? How many victims had he fleeced in the past and what number was I.

22

Hellhound on My Trail

After the wedding, I never went back home. I was staying in Surrey with my brother Tom at his girlfriend's house in a location Jamie didn't know. I was advised to stay far away from my house and contact the police in a different county and see what they could do. Jamie was still bombarding me with texts and unwilling to go lightly. I had tried several times before getting rid of him but he just turned back up on my doorstep. Everything was in tatters. I felt worthless and was wading through a dark, future-less life. Between the stress of the divorce, spiralling debits and heartache, I barely had any energy to make it through each day, but I had to keep it together. At least, I had the peace and tranquillity of Tom's lovely house and garden for a few weeks. This whole time I was having to listen to Jamie's endless whiney voice messages and emails and I was calling the police daily. They said Jamie had not committed a crime since I had been willingly giving him money and I had no address for him to get a caution for harassing me.

After I spoke to the police, they advised me to go to Epsom Police Station and make a formal statement. I dreaded going to the police station and having to dredge up all the awful, shameful details of my life. Maybe I'd just rather not be reminded. Considering I had been sectioned, I was afraid they wouldn't take me seriously and dismiss me as just a time-wasting nutter. The woman taking my statement looked at me. I could see her staring at me, assessing me, how I spoke, and what I was wearing. She asked me if he was forcing me to have sex with him. If he was abusing me, obviously he wasn't, but mentally and financially he certainly was. I sat there feeling sick and scared to death. They advised me to email him, saying "no further contact", and if he continued harassing me, he would be breaching the caution. He never stopped calling and sent a flurry of emails, so I emailed, as the police instructed, telling him to back off and I wished to have no further contact with him.

From the first moment I told Sara about Jamie, she knew instantly that he was a fraudster and conman. Her biggest fear was that he might be dangerous and would hurt me. It never crossed my mind. Because of the unusual situation of being sectioned, I actually felt sorry for him. How had my life gotten so fucked up? From a stable marriage and children on the way to nothing, no one and I had fallen for yet another liar and manipulator.

Towards the end of our time together, I had seen how ugly Jamie was beginning to look, and he had lost a tooth and was no longer that lovely-looking man I had once seen through rose- tinted glasses, but an ugly, menacing creature who was demanding and manipulative. He looked worn-out and ill, with his sweaty skin and sunken cheeks. Oh my God, I had even believed he was spiritual. As well as living off me, the list of items he had convinced me to buy him ranged from clothes, shoes, and grooming products to an iPhone (he had nagged me to get him a contract since day one, thank god I had refused him but finally succumbed to buy a second hand one), countless restaurant meals and hotels. I must've been bonkers, or he must've been a fantastic liar and skilled swindler. He had done a wonderful job on me—this was beyond catfishing— but targeting weak and wounded prey that could be taken down easily. I was a vulnerable, grief-stricken woman who had lost her husband, her children, and her connection to her family and friends—the perfect candidate to scam and steal from. I was embarrassed by the mess I had got myself into. All I wanted was to be cared for during a terrible time and he didn't even do that. Everything was all about him and fulfilling his needs I had completely lost all sense of myself.

During our time together we had been listening to the album by Sam Smith in the car and ironically the first track was Money on my Mind. I had spent the last month with only money on my mind, worrying about debts and wondering if he was ever paying me back. My anxiety was sky high and I had been clinging to life by my fingernails. If I had died there and then it would have been a godsend.

Early on, I remember wanting to call the police to get rid of him as he clung to me at every moment. Instead, I had got swept away with a calculating bastard and complete idiot, just like my ex. At least Andy had a responsible job and was an upstanding member of society. Once again, I felt abused. I wasn't sure if I could trust the police but needed their protection.

The last few days in Surrey, Jamie had blackmailed me, threatening to go to my mother's house or my husband's place of work if I didn't meet with him. I knew I had to learn something from this cringy, soul-sapping experience. I had to write a book—no one would believe it was true—and I had to help others. I knew other people must get themselves into this kind of nightmarish position. At least now I had gotten out of it. I knew I would survive. I couldn't possibly kill myself and let that lying, parasitic loser of an ex-husband get all the money from the house. I had to stay alive long enough to sort that out. Now I was not only being bullied by my ex-husband, but by my ex-friend from the loony bin.

As expected, the police didn't take me seriously. This was romance fraud, in which they took little interest and typically there was no recourse as proving criminal activity was extremely difficult. After a week, I was suddenly called to be interviewed at yet another police station in the same city as the psych ward. I had to make a statement and take the few pieces of his belongings which he had purposely left with me.

I drove the three hours from Surrey to Southampton. I felt empty, worthless and incredibly stupid. The police must have thought what an idiot to have fallen for this obvious con man. My dreams of finding some future happiness had been projected onto this man and I only saw what I had wanted to see. I had 'visioned' him into being. It made me realise how ridiculous I had been to be so easily manipulated. I spent over four long hours giving a comprehensive statement talking about my disastrous life.

After that I drove back and halfway to Surrey, I realised the engine was starting to overheat and my phone battery was dying. It was already dark. I stopped at a garage for help. If I broke down on the motorway, I was scared I would be stranded without a working phone. The shop assistant at the petrol station wouldn't let me use his phone but pointed to the hotel behind it. I broke down in tears and wandered to the hotel. The kind lady at reception not only allowed me to use the phone but, seeing my distress, sorted out a cup of coffee and charged up my phone. I called Sara and cried on the phone. My car and I had now both broken down. I sat down in the tiny hotel lobby and the receptionist brought over a coffee and biscuits.

Even the mechanic who turned up and collected my keys was jolly and had some compassion. He told me to relax and drink my coffee while he finished mending my car. Teary and exhausted, I was incredibly touched and grateful for these small kindnesses.

The receptionist told me her daughter would react exactly the same and refused any payment for the coffee. By now, as it was too late to drive back to Surrey, I stayed alone in my spooky, unlived-in house. I knew I had to go back home at some point and had the locks changed again. How could my normal life end up in such a mess, trauma on top of trauma? I existed in an almost constant state of paranoia, worrying if Andy could show up at any moment or that Jamie was lurking around in the shadows waiting to ambush me.

I felt very angry with myself, how had it come to this? How

could I be so stupid to trust a man I met in a mental ward? Guess I had been in a very vulnerable place and was open to manipulation. I just hadn't realised it. Jamie knew all about my family and friends. I thought I knew all about him but in actual fact everything he told me was a preposterous lie. I was surprised he didn't tell me he was dying of cancer too. He was an imposter who'd drawn me in so beautifully. What stung the hardest was the shame of being duped and strung along for so long.

And now I had to agree to go to court to press charges, only to find out that his small-time grifting was a lengthy criminal career. No one was safe from Jamie. He had been scamming people professionally for some time. One way, was by getting checked into a hospital and finding vulnerable people to defraud them out of money. I was just one of many.

At least for the moment, I was temporarily safe and sleeping again. I had people around me too and no one had my brother's address. My car broke down again so I was stuck in Surrey for a bit longer until I could get back on my feet. Three weeks later I was still getting emails from Jamie begging to speak with me and that he only wanted to give me the money that was rightfully mine. He needed to see me in person though. I breathed a sigh of relief, here I could pretend to be normal for a bit. I could forget about my house for a while, knowing my lovely neighbours were keeping an eye on it.

Thank God it was sunny and I could lie on the sun lounger in my brother's garden and relax by the pond. If nothing else, I had to scrape through this with my sanity intact. Sara was angry with me and Marcus and Stephanie were disappointed, but they knew why this had happened. It was a direct result of how my husband had treated me. They didn't want me to fall apart six months down the line. Here I was suffering yet again because of another deceitful arsehole. This time I was going to learn from it. My sister lent me money to pay off my debts to get me out of this temporary mess. I would never have trusted someone like Jamie under normal circumstances. Although saying that, I had trusted my husband with our savings and he put all our money in his own account. There was no happy-ever-after to this relationship. Just fear, anxiety and debt. I understood now how women can be taken in by charming, persuasive men and be fleeced for everything. This had been different but with the same result.

During this short, screwed-up, six-month relationship with Jamie, I felt trapped and, for the first time ever, I was scrambling to find a reason to live. Soon I would be losing my home, too. I had no proper job and was waist-deep in debt with no way of repaying them, in addition to the enormous guilt of upsetting my whole family.

I was determined to survive this temporary situation and no one, especially a man, would get to ruin my life again. Even Luke, my ex-boyfriend of 14 years, had let me down spectacularly. While my father was on his deathbed, he had nipped off and had an affair. He had been flirting with some woman while I was away looking after my dying father. He wasn't interested in death, although he managed to write enough songs about it.

Bless him, he wasn't a happy man. When we were touring Europe with the Auteurs, Luke had a mental breakdown, and couldn't handle the stress of touring and playing the same songs every night. He got to a point he could barely talk to the other band members. He was getting paranoid and more difficult than usual. I supported him and we eventually got through all the dates in France and made it to Spain.

One night, happy to have finished the French leg of the tour, we were celebrating having made it to San Sebastián. After a few drinks and only tapas for dinner, we all walked home along the promenade. The roadies decided to climb a steep ten-foot wall down to the beach. I watched my boyfriend, who was hardly athletic, astounded by the sheer madness he was contemplating. I stood by the railing, shouting to him, "Luke, stop... Don't do it. Please STOP!" Either he couldn't hear me or was blinded by alcohol. I watched in horror as he took the huge jump straight onto the concrete below. In a moment he landed, like a felled tree flat on his back, and kept trying to get up. He couldn't stand up, staggering and stumbling backwards. The three roadies rushed towards him and in their drunken stupor carried him back up to the promenade.

They got him back to the hotel room and left it to me to sort him out. I went down to reception to get a bucket of ice to numb the pain in his ankles. All night long, he was in crippling pain. Then, we were off to the hospital for X-rays and he was given painkillers and crutches for his broken ankle. By the time we got back to the UK, a few days later, we went to another hospital, where two broken ankles were diagnosed and one needed significant surgery to rebuild it. Suffice to say, he spent the next three months crawling around the house on his knees and I was nursing him back to health. He barely left the house and, when he did, he was in a wheelchair. Meanwhile, he spent most of his time in bed, happily writing a new album. And, of course, despite everything, he would betray me.

I often wondered how I ended up with such losers. It had taken me years to recover from that long-term relationship and find a decent man. I thought I had found that man in Andy. How wrong I had been with my disastrous choice of men.

23

Begin Again: April 2015

I was slowly waking up to my new reality. For a long time, I had to keep it a secret, fearing my family would never trust me again and possibly send me back inside. Either way, I couldn't take that risk. I had so many complaints to make: the clinic; the adoption agency; the rubbish solicitors; my latest solicitor. All the first solicitor did was support my husband and sent me a huge bill.

Beyond being burnt out and at breaking point, I had to find a counsellor who I could talk to and click with. Thankfully, I got a recommendation. She lived near my mother and came highly recommended by two separate members of my family. Since I had been committed, a care-in-the-community person was supposed to check up on me. They weren't prepared to offer any counselling since I hadn't been suicidal. They advised going back to my doctor. The last thing I was going to do. I'd had enough of doctors and drugs.

Carol, a tall, slender well-spoken woman, had previously spent her career working in the City of London, in the competitive world of business. Besides retraining as a counsellor, she had trained in EMDR therapy (Eye Movement Desensitization Reprocessing), which is good for PTSD and trauma. The whole experience of being held captive and drugged, kicked out and preyed upon by a swindler had left me battered and broken. I needed to let go of the trauma of my past to rebuild my life anew.

On our first session, I knocked on her door and entered her Victorian terraced house. She greeted me with a smile and led me into a spacious lounge room. As I told her my long and dramatic story, I couldn't stop crying. I felt deeply ashamed by my circumstances. I noticed she spent a lot of her time with her hand over her heart as if protecting herself from my awful story. She gave me some valuable advice. She said I had a "normal reaction to an abnormal situation", which could plunge an otherwise normal person's life into chaos. I had finally found someone who could help me get out of my totally messed-up situation.

Each week I visited her and spoke of my problems, often in tears. It was as if I had waited all week to allow my emotions to flow. I told her while inside the psychiatric unit, I had met Jamie, and only had recently unceremoniously dumped him, like my husband had dumped me. She didn't know the full story and seemed to take the side of Jamie. I couldn't bring myself to tell her that he was a fraudster who had duped me into giving him money for six months. I now had parking fees coming through the door, and more unknowns for me to manage. It brought it home to me and gave me proof that the 'business trips' were all lies. I had been having a mini nervous breakdown daily as I couldn't take it anymore.

I had moved back home again and was constantly fearful that Andy or Jamie would turn up. I kept changing rooms around the house to see where I could sleep and ended up sleeping on the sofa. I never slept in our marital bed again or even entered the room we once shared. It was creepy, like a tomb of some past tragedy. It got so bad at one point, when I was monitoring my blood pressure, it was over 200. At 1:30 am, I called Kathy, who was back in the UK visiting from Nepal as my heart was beating too loudly and I couldn't sleep. In an aim to return to my pre-crisis life, I was applying for jobs and had an interview the following day. My body couldn't cope with the stress of it all. Both my arms were numb and I was worried I was going to have a stroke.

At the end of the phone conversation I had with Sara, she said, "What's the worst thing that can happen? You will die."

And I said, "Well, I wouldn't mind dying. I just want to get rid of the constant pain."

Not sleeping was tolerable. It was the constant panic about not breathing, my heart clattering and my sky-high blood pressure. I was measuring it a few times a day to try and keep it under control. I knew I needed to calm down but wasn't sure how. I'd never, under any circumstances, call an ambulance after the nightmare experience of being locked up. I would rather die. I made it through the night, but it was a long one, lying on the sofa, with Kathy on the other sofa nearby, keeping a watchful eye on me.

Thinking positive thoughts was so important, but difficult when I spent most of my waking hours living in fear. I longed for a quiet and simple life. How could I help others and myself? How do other people get out of terrible messes like this? I had my vision board, but after what happened last time, I didn't want to vision anything else. I wanted to see the Dalai Lama and I had already had a blessing from Mother Meera. I hoped to get a hug from Mother Amma, when she was over in the UK again. My idea was by getting all these spiritual blessings my life would improve. I hoped to start over, move to another country and live by the sea. I needed someone to love and care for. Maybe a dog and a cat or two?

I had to begin again and with the help of people like Byron Katie (question every thought), Eckhart Tolle (staying in the now moment) and the Dalai Lama (an inspiration for boundless peace and compassion). I knew I had to do something and to help other people.

In a moment of clarity, instead of fighting my way through this experience as everything continued to crumble around me, I decided to let go of that life, and forgive everyone, especially my ex-husband, as being bitter and angry only caused me more pain. I didn't complain to anyone or the organisation, as it was pointless. I focused all my energy on regaining my health by doing a daily kundalini yoga session on my own at home. I practised breathing techniques to calm my overloaded nervous system.

Later, after taking Ayurvedic classes, I sought out a lovely Ayurveda doctor who gave me the herbs and routines I needed to bring me back to myself and balance my overactive nervous system. Slowly but surely, my health began to improve. At times, I dreamt about finding a partner and, if it didn't happen that was fine too. I had to work on my self-esteem, love myself and find something meaningful in my life.

My new dreams of living by the sea in sunnier climes were not just a bit of fantasy. I had been to plenty of far-flung countries and knew it was all possible. I longed to travel again, seeing beautiful places to inspire me. First, I worked on sorting out my health until I was well enough. I was on a quest to find a new home, a new country and a new life far away from the dreary UK.

24

Finding Blessings

I was standing in a football stadium of all places, and 30 feet away from me was the Dalai Lama himself. I wondered for a moment if I was dreaming. He stood in a ray of sunlight, deepening the rich colours of his purple, red and yellow robes, the Buddhist icon himself. The audience that has been patiently waiting for over half an hour, all eyes were upon the small, skinny man draped in his colourful robes. With just one smile from the Tibetan spiritual leader, the audience and I was captivated by his every word. It felt like the whole audience was connected, we were united in these moments together within the sacred light of the Dalai Lama.

Many people talked about the Dalai Lama's magical presence and they were right. I could energetically feel the blessing just being in his presence and frequency. I pinched myself, amazed to be here, fulfilling the dream I had last year when I was feeling at my lowest point. It gave me a sense that my healing and recovery are possible.

I felt so unlucky with my whole situation, the Dalai Lama had given me so much hope, just knowing how much he served others and being such a compassionate human being inspired me. I decided I would get blessed as much as possible, maybe this could cleanse me of my past. I had researched where the Dalai Lama was going to give his talks, at this time it was mainly in Scandinavia. I couldn't face leaving the UK as my health wasn't yet fully back to normal and I was easily panicked. One day by a stroke of luck, I saw that the Dalai Lama was going to be in Hampshire, where I was living. He was going to be presenting a talk in a small stadium in Aldershot of all places. I don't like stadiums, but this was a small open-air one and I knew this was my chance to be in his presence. I booked my ticket online there and then.

The day arrived in June 2015, as it was in the afternoon I took my time and drove the hour-and-half trip to Aldershot. I felt excited to finally have a dream come true. I had been reading his book The Art of Happiness and had benefitted so much from reading it. When I neared the venue in Aldershot, I was surprised to see a demonstration going on outside. There was a small group of angry people, handing out leaflets and chanting: "Dalai Lama stop lying." I passed through the crowd and found a small park with a patch of grass to sit down and relax for a while. That's all I needed, people shouting about corruption and dishonesty. It made me a bit anxious and stressed, but I was here now and I wanted to see and feel his energy. When it was time, I slowly walked back to the venue to pick up my ticket. When I came out of the kiosk, the Dalai Lama was getting out of a car and walked straight past me. I felt blessed to see him so close. It made my day no matter what happened next.

As I entered the stadium and found the section I was allowed to sit in, I met Tara, a lovely jolly Scottish woman. We instantly connected and started chatting. Tara seemed excited too. She had flown down from Scotland especially and had seen him many times. She told me she usually cries when she first sees him, feeling so overwhelmed.

When he appeared, I could feel his energy, he exuded serenity and peace all around him. At times we struggled to hear him over the chanting and shouting outside the venue. I was overcome with sadness for their reactions, but seeing him felt like a small miracle. I had come here all on my own and had the courage to follow my dream and be in a stadium with hundreds of people. Afterwards, my new Scottish friend and I went and had coffee and cake to celebrate our Dalai Lama day.

The last time I recall being in a huge stadium was the Stade De France in Paris for a rugby game with my husband with a ridiculous amount of people. When we left and made it to the metro, I had a sudden panic attack. Admittedly, this was a much smaller venue, but I had been fine and completed my mission of feeling blessed.

As I hadn't fully benefited from seeing the Dalai Lama, I found he had another event happening at the Excel Centre in London. I went to see him again. This time it was inside a closed space and the protesters couldn't get in and disturb the peace of listening to the Dalai Lama. There was also a Tibetan man singing and playing a local traditional stringed instrument, which was hauntingly beautiful. I thought the Dalai Lama was looking old and seemed a little sad. Maybe it was me, but I was glad I had made the effort.

I was going to get as many blessings as I could. I had a lot to heal and clear myself of my grief and personal turmoil, what better way of helping me than being blessed. After being locked up, I applied for my spiritual name as a celebration I had survived. I knew I had to find a more meaningful path now. You can apply through the 3HO Foundation for a spiritual name and the one chosen for me was very apt, Mantra Simran Kaur. Mantra is a vibration that nurtures the soul. It is God's phone number. Simran means to practice meditation, remembering God's Name in your heart and on your lips with every breath. In essence, it means that whenever you call on God, your soul radiates. Kaur means lioness - all women were given this name.

I'd heard of a spiritual guru called Mother Amma, along with Mother Meera who I had already received a blessing from and I thought maybe a blessing from Amma, too, could help me along my journey of healing.

Mother Meera, a mystic and the divine embodiment of the sacred feminine, heals and transforms others by silence, touch or sight. A farm girl born in southern India in 1960, she lived simply in a village outside Frankfurt, Germany, where eager seekers made pilgrimages from around the globe to see her. She travelled around Europe, America and Canada, giving darshans to anyone who wishes to receive one. She believes her mission on earth is to prepare humanity for spiritual transformation.

When you enter the darshan space, everyone is silent, and you sit and wait until it's your turn to get a blessing from her. When it was my time, I slowly walked up to the stage shuffling on my knees. I sat opposite her at her feet, and leaned my head downwards. The darshan is a simple ritual where she holds your head lightly in her hands to untangle energetic knots. She had a lovely aura of peace, and was in deep meditation as she transmitted her frequency to me. When she finished, she gently removed her hands and I looked into her eyes for a moment in gratitude. I found the space calming, sitting quietly and watching people receive a darshan felt very serene and took me to a place of peace.

Mother Amma was quite a different experience. The atmosphere was very buzzy and joyful with people singing. Born in Kerala, India in 1953, Mata Amritanandamayi Devi, known as Amma or 'mother', is a Hindu guru and humanitarian, revered as 'the hugging saint' by her followers and has hugged over 38 million people. She runs a massive charity in Kerala. I went to see her at Alexander Palace in London, not knowing what to expect. The vibe was very different to what I had imagined after seeing Mother Meera. She sat on the stage, with her followers around her, and when you go up to her, she embraces you with a huge hug. I could feel the power of her embrace and felt quite emotional but also reassured by her magnificent aura. Afterwards she discreetly places a sweet and flower in the palm of your hand and sends you on your way. It was uplifting and joyful being in the happy atmosphere.

Alongside these pilgrimages to see spiritual people, I was working on my health and seeing an Ayurvedic doctor who was also a cancer consultant in a local NHS hospital. At the same time, he was running courses on learning about holistic health, mainly

Ayurveda but also about longevity and the blue zones. Dr Sam Watts was amazing and one of the first people I was able to talk to about my traumas without feeling judged. He suggested detoxing my body from the medication. During the course, they also advise you to find your ikigai or your reason for living. Which for me at the time was challenging, as I had to find a whole new purpose in life. I could only dream of getting healthy, going travelling again and seeing the beauty of the world. I held onto that dream and created a new vision board made up of places I had wanted to see and experiences I wanted to have.

I had been working for Linda Jarrett, a healer and clairvoyant for some years creating graphic design material and promoting her business. She had been the one who had told me I had a past life with my daughter Isabella. She channelled the information and supported me through my adoption journey. During the years I had worked for her, I had built a strong relationship with her and her husband Chris. I would support her at her workshops and over the years she would give me many readings. She said that sometimes we have to go through these transformational events or traumas to get us on our spiritual path, a normal process of awakening the soul and getting us onto our truest way of living. She gave me hope that things would improve and that this was my life path. During this period, I continued to journal about my life and create small books, as finding some creative expression was essential. I had always loved photography and made sure I took photos to inspire me. I worked on listening to my body, and what it needed, and created a daily routine to support me. I wrote a list of all the things I loved to do such as being in nature, singing, walking along the beach and doing yoga. Above all, I had to work on letting go of fear and finding peace in my heart by meditating, singing mantra and learning to live in the moment. Little by little, I could find more joy and love each day. I had to understand that everyone lives with the unknown, and it was only my reaction to it that would determine my life and how I chose to live it.

I started to love myself by doing what my body, mind and soul needed. Most of all, it was about being kind to myself and nurturing myself back to health. I started with forgiving others, accepting the challenges I had gone through, and being grateful I was still here. I could start over again—not knowing where that would be, but trusting I would be guided along the way. I had the insight I was meant to experience what had happened to me and that it would lead me on my path to freedom. As time passed, I gained clarity in my life, gently moving forward and rebuilding my relationships with friends and family. Learning to trust myself again and others around me. This was going to be key in rebuilding my lost confidence and finding the courage to create a new direction.

25

A Voyage of Discovery

I always believed every one has a purpose and that it's a matter of finding it. The phrase 'what you seek is seeking you' by Rumi, the 13th-century Persian philosopher and poet, is a beautiful way of seeing the world. Those simple yet undeniably mystical words were imbued with so much potency. I knew I had to listen to my intuition and my heart to find what was meant for me. It took longer than expected to sort out my life and prepare to follow my new dream of travelling. My sister Kathy had spent many years living in Nepal. I had visited her once in Pokhara, where she was mainly based. I can vividly remember the first moment I landed there and stood by the lake feeling a sense of being in a place I'd been before. I could feel the peace and serenity of this beautiful country, the lake mirroring the magnificent mountain range.

I first visited in 2008 when I was in India, with my friend Cleo, a graphic designer who worked with me on various magazines at IPC Media (Time Inc). A slightly crazy redhead, Cleo could be a bit wild at times but bags of fun. One day at work we spontaneously decided we would meet some friends who were in Goa and take a second week and journey across land from Goa to Nepal. It was a long and exhausting trip, including two long train rides. On the second train journey overnight from Varanasi, I had a panic attack. Being locked in a small two-bedded cabin, with no access to opening the window for air, just a grey metal sheet, I felt trapped, but I had made it through by focusing on my breath. We took an overloaded bus trip at night going across the mountains and even a horse and cart ride to get to immigration from across the border. Only a two-week holiday, it was a real adventure, fitting in this trip across land. Nepal is a place that calls you back and nourishes your soul by just being on the land.

So here I was once again. I had landed in Kathmandu this time, where we visited some of the ancient cities of Patan and Bandipur. Seeing the beautiful old architecture, it was like being in another land, otherworldly and far away from western civilisation. Walking around the dusty streets of Kathmandu and hearing the constant sounds of mantra, the well-known Buddhist mantra, Om mani padme hum brought back many memories of my previous visits. I felt at home again. I would go around all day singing the soothing mantra in my head. It brought me to a place of peace. In Nepal, singing and hearing mantra every day was normal and part of the reason why I felt so at home. The place spoke to my soul.

It was a relief to have finally left the UK and be on a new life journey to find a place to call home. After a few days of rediscovering Kathmandu, we took a taxi across to Pokhara, the place had changed so much since my first visit in 2008. My sister Kathy had been doing Ayurvedic treatments in a local clinic, so she booked me in for a two-week Panchakarma program. Living in a clinic was a big experience and reminded me of my time being locked up and alone. Sometimes the daily schedule of massages and other treatments made me feel trapped and emotional. But the staff were amazing and Dr Rishi, a diminutive and wise man who gave me the initial consultation, was empathetic and supportive. I wasn't used to this kindness and didn't want to draw any extra attention to myself, but after five days with a headache, the place was getting to me. I had to reach out and ask for help, and Dr Rishi was on the end of the phone one night to talk me through how I felt and apparently, it was a normal process for everyone. The clinic was a family business, Dr Rishi's brother Badrai ran the business side in partnership with a German woman Marlies. Together they were like a family. I remember one time after I had left, they invited us to a party and insisted we all danced. Dr Rishi told me that dancing was key to having a happier life. I definitely needed to fit more music, dancing and laughter into my new life.

A friend of the family was visiting Nepal at the same time. I felt lucky we could be at the clinic together. I had someone around that was going through a similar process for the first time too. I didn't know Jane well, but she seemed kind and gentle. A tall slender woman, with short blonde hair, she was from the north of England and had a sweet Yorkshire accent. We made the most of our time high up in the hills with the view of Pokhara and the glimmering lake below. We got to know each other and shared our personal challenges and stories. On the final day, of the Panchakarma treatment, you have a rebirthing ceremony. This entails being massaged by five or more people at once, and then a bath with flowers laid out on the floor in your name. These rituals signify the beginning of a new path.

Afterwards, we spent some time in the mountains, seeing the Annapurna range. This was another adventure climbing up steep hillsides, breathless, but it was all worth it for the views of some of the most breathtaking scenery in the world. Being high up in the mountains in such a close connection with nature felt liberating and expansive. This alone gave me a renewed sense of optimism. We took a few trips and stayed in local homestays, which usually meant living in cute little wooden houses. It felt like staying in Little Red Riding Hood's house, incredibly chilly though. We all were bundled up in all our clothes since we hadn't come prepared for the high-altitude chill of the mountains. Seeing the sun rise over the snow-crested peaks of the Himalayas felt so special and lifted me into another space and time, my past bad experiences in the UK seemed to melt away. I felt so good travelling and spending time with Kathy and Jane. I was on a mission to be inspired by the wonders of nature and the special energy of Nepal. I could start to let go of the past and start living more in the present. It gave me a sense that now my life was finally about to change.

My sister had many friends in Pokhara, and we were welcomed by the women who ran the Three Sisters Trekking company, all their nieces and extended family and friends. Being around a community of people made our time much more fun. We spent many hours drinking tea and hot chocolate at a small café owned by a lovely local family my sister had connected with. It was a simpler but richer way of living that felt worlds away from my old life in the UK. I had to start rewriting my future and Nepal was a good place to start. After a few months in Nepal, we decided to travel around southern India together. Kathy wanted to fit in a trip to Calcutta, so Jane and I were going to meet her in Chennai, and spend a bit more time in Nepal.

When we arrived at Chennai airport on 5 December 2016, it had been announced that evening that Jayaram Jayalalithaa, the 68-year-old chief minister of Tamil Nadu, had suddenly died of a heart attack. The whole city was in turmoil and there were no taxis. Chennai, also known as Madras, the capital of Tamil Nadu, was at a standstill and there was talk of riots going on around the city. Thousands of police had been deployed to maintain the mass hysteria and outpourings of grief. If you don't know much about Tamil Nadu, it's known for people being quite fanatical at times. We had booked our hotel quite centrally where hundreds of thousands of people from all over Tamil Nadu had descended on the city to pay their respects to her. Jayalalithaa was a big celebrity, who had been an actress in her younger days and challenged the state's male-dominated politics. She went on to become the chief minister for a quarter of a century and a much-loved progressive figure, known for her generous welfare policies, including distributing meals to the poor, who inspired cult-like devotion. She also pioneered alternative energy and water-harvesting schemes, as well as reducing female infanticide by creating centres where parents could anonymously hand over unwanted baby girls. Equally, she was imperious, a ruthless autocrat who could never shake off accusations of corruption.

After an hour of slogging around the airport, we finally found a taxi that would take us to a local hotel. Kathy was very nervous since there wasn't one driver but two, which felt wrong, so we immediately jumped out of the taxi and found another. This one took us to a hotel, and we managed to get two rooms. We were advised that it was best we just locked ourselves in the hotel for a few days until things settled down. The hotel was okay, it felt a bit grey and dingy, but we were grateful to be safe and the Indian food was amazing. There wasn't much we could do but lie low and read a book.

There was no traffic for days, so we stayed in the hotel or wandered around a few nearby empty streets, while the whole centre of the city was descended upon apparently, but we never saw Chennai itself. All we saw were deserted streets and the odd cow crossing the road. There was a general feeling of tension and energy of anticipation as we waited in our holding pad until it was safe to move onwards on our journey. On top of this, the government had taken a common note out of circulation making it difficult for locals and foreigners to exchange money and get any cash out. The cash limit was around the equivalent of 15 pounds a day. So, we spent every day trying to find ATMs and queueing for hours to get a tiny bit of cash. Luckily my sister Kathy was organised and had a stash of money that we could all share until the situation improved, and then we could pay her back. What I remembered most about this trip was queueing endlessly for cash and teaching local Indians how to use cashpoint machines. They had to cash in their money to the banks and were given cards but many hadn't used one before. It was a big step in digitalising the currency in India.

A few days passed hiding out in our hotel which was called MARS. It certainly felt like we had landed on another planet. We escaped to the nearest coastal town, where we had some freedom. Malappuram had a laid-back seaside town feel with the most amazing stone carvings everywhere. I bought myself a small carved Buddha with a carving of a hand on the back, a small treasure to remind me of that trip.

While in Malappuram I had the realisation that I had all the answers and the pain in my arms that I had for the last few years was to awaken me to my path of writing my own story. I was also carrying a guilty secret that I couldn't share with anyone; the police were in contact with me regularly updating me about finding Jamie. The shame and humiliation I felt was lying heavily on my shoulders. Marcus was the only one I was able to talk about it with, but I didn't want to burden him since he and Stephanie had helped me enough already. The policewoman, Jan, was amazing and would call me every couple of weeks to give me an update. I dreaded her calls, fearful of what she was going to tell me next. One evening she rang with some shocking news. She told me I wasn't the only one Jamie had extorted. They had found 22 other people (mostly women but some men too), whom they had interviewed. It brought me some relief, but knowing that they wanted me to appear in court in the UK was another stress I could do without.

After a few days in Malappuram relaxing, taking in the sea air and visiting local tourist sites, we moved on and left just in time to miss Cyclone Vardah. It had crossed the eastern coast of Chennai and had ripped through Malappuram, yet another lucky escape. The next stop was Pondicherry, a French colonial city by the sea and the home of Sri Aurobindo, an Indian philosopher, yoga guru, maharishi and poet.

We took several trips there and visited the Matramandir, a huge magnificent building with a shining gold dome in an expanse of flat red desert, which felt like it was out of this world. When you entered Matramandir, inside it was completely white and you had to wear white socks. It was like stepping inside a spaceship and everyone walked silently in single file to the inner sanctum, a white cylindrical room with very high ceilings. Silence was required all the time and when you entered the inner room, you found a place to sit on the floor around the edges of the room. In the centre, there was a large spherical quartz crystal that you could look at or just close your eyes and relax. It was incredibly uplifting being there. Sometimes I could see faces in the crystal and I received messages during these sessions. When I returned to our lodgings, I would draw what I had seen on small square pieces of paper and express the feelings, I had felt while in meditation. It was such a beautiful experience drawing in the energy of peace, spaciousness and nothingness. I could imagine myself living here if I couldn't find a home elsewhere.

Auroville, a progressive town in Pondicherry, was an international community dedicated to peace, sustainability and divine consciousness. Tucked into a jungle of trees, this self-styled utopia was filled with gorgeous whitewashed colonial buildings and cobbled streets, and was considered the French Riviera of the East. One day during our visit we took part in an art class, where we created our own mala beads from a single piece of paper. We painted our vision or what we wanted for the future onto the paper using words and images. We then cut the paper up into thin strips and made our own beads from the paper. I always had a strong connection with mala beads as I had been doing my daily mantra for over two years. It had been a tool to support me through my spiritual awakening, and life generally. Now I had created my own unique mala bracelet.

While in Pondicherry we planned our trip to travel across all the main temples in southern India. We were pilgrims following the well-worn route of many others and feeling the energy of the temples, all built on ley lines, where the natural energy of power lies. Our first stop was Chidambaram, to see the colourful and ornate Nataraja Temple, dedicated to Lord Shiva. It was a whirlwind tour across the country culminating in a temple in Kanyakumari off the tip of India. I was able to photograph all the places which had become a passion of mine since the mid-90s.

In India, I came across Inner Engineering: A Yogi's Guide to Joy by Sadhguru. I loved this book and for months I sang his mantra called the Isha Kriya: I am not the body, I am not even the mind. The powerful mantra brings you into a state of relaxation and realisation. I chanted it for 30 days and found peace within.

Our last stop in India was Varkala, a town on a clifftop with a sandy beach below. Backed by palm-fringed red cliffs, the beach was famous for priests who sat on the sand and performed ceremonies for people who had died. Before leaving, I wanted to do a ceremony for my dad. I had been eyeing up all the wise old-looking priests. When I went down to the beach, a young priest, whose energy was full of life, called me over. He was in his 20s or 30s and had deep dark skin, with the kindest eyes and an exuberant smile. During the ceremony which seemed to last for ages, he got me to chant with him. It was a long and complicated mantra but somehow it flowed out of me as if I already knew it. I took an offering for my dad to the sea that we had prayed over. Then he gave me a set of wooden mala beads and told me to chant Om Namah Shivaya. I felt emotional honouring my dad, but was pleased I had taken the time for remembrance. My dad had his ashes scattered into the sea in the UK, back in 1999, so it felt like he had come full circle.

While in Varkala, Marion, another designer friend from London who I had worked with on several women's glossies at IPC Media, came to visit. A tall beautiful, stylish woman, with bright blue eyes and long dark hair with a fringe, Marion had the sweetest of smiles and spoke with a lovely soft Dundee accent. She was full of fun and mischief, and we got to connect and be silly like the old days. Marion was also an angel in disguise as she was one of the few people I had mentioned Jamie, the sociopath to. I felt lucky and grateful she was there at the time to support me and help me write the letter to the court. In the end, I didn't need to attend the hearing since Jamie had pleaded guilty and so his sentence had been cut in half. I was now going to be able to release the past fully. Marion and I had lots of fun and laughs during her time in India, and it was a welcome relief to have a long-standing friend around whom I could connect and share fun times with.

Time flew by and my visa was running out. I had to decide on my next move. I didn't feel I wanted to go back to Nepal, as I didn't feel it was my place. I had to keep on searching for my home and to branch off alone. Jane was going back to the UK and my sister had returned to another part of India.

After writing a wish list of the places, I had wanted to go to: Hawaii, Sedona, Mexico, Bali came up as the next place for me to go.

26

Bali Brings Me Home

The decision was made and once again I returned to Bali in February 2017. I headed to Canggu, staying in Serenity Eco Guesthouse in a quiet street near the beach. I immediately connected with some fellow travellers. A tall handsome flight attendant from Brazil, now living in the US, and a cool young French girl. Bali felt safe and a relaxing place for me to be. I saw a cat-sitting offer on social media and got in touch with the woman. Originally from New Zealand, Lynn asked me to cat-and-rabbit sit for a few weeks in a beautiful house in a village just outside of Canggu . It felt like my life had started to open up to new opportunities, so I knew I was in the right place, as it seemed to be working out with perfect synchronicity.

On my first visit to Ubud, I found the town hectic and overwhelming, so unlike how I had remembered it back in 2001. I could hardly recognise the place, it felt too fast-paced for me. It took a few visits to realise that the town has many layers. The energy calls you back as you discover new layers—it lets you in or kicks you out. This time around it felt right and so I moved to Ubud. It was around the time Mount Agung was sending strong signals of potentially going off, which brought much fear to Ubud and the island as a whole. Although we were 30km away from Mount Agung, we did feel quite a few earthquakes and sometimes a thin layer of volcanic dust would land on bikes and cars.

One morning when I was sitting on my bed, I looked up at the ceiling and saw it was pulsating and moving. I could feel the tremors shaking through my bed and beneath me. After a few seconds, I got out of the room. I could hear some local people screaming when I walked outside. I thought to myself, we're all in this trauma together. I am not alone. It brought me to a place of acceptance, knowing we can only control our reactions to life. Sure, it was a shock, but part of life, nature has its way of communicating. Indonesia lies on a ring of fire and so this was bound to happen from time to time. I had to get used to it if I was going to live here.

One of the things I discovered in Bali was sound healing. I took many trips to the Pyramids of Chi, where I met many good friends over the years. On my first session, I met Didi, a sound healer and a beautiful soul. Going regularly to sound healing, I was able to release the pain in my body. I met the fabulous owner's Peter and Lynn and learnt about their story of being called to Bali to build the Pyramids. They were always finding stray or dumped puppies nearby and would care for them and rehome them all. A few times I would dog-sit for Lynn and Peter as I found caring for animals a way to connect back to nature and myself. I also met another long-standing friend at the Pyramids of Chi one evening, Yuni, a sweet Balinese woman who lived in Ubud with her husband. Soon after meeting, we started catching up for coffee, visiting temples and going on adventures around Bali and becoming good friends.

A well-known local tarot reader in Ubud, called Noviana Kusumawardhani told me I could live in Bali and call it home. She suggested I visited one of the oldest temples, Pura Puncak Penulisan. She told me I had been a priest in a past life during the time this temple was created, and she suggested I go and pay my respects. I went there with Yuni and my Finnish friend Anna Liisa. As we travelled up towards Mount Batur in Kintamani to the temple, the rain came lashing down. It poured down the 300 steps up to the Temple and turned into a temporary water temple for us. Before going up the steps, the three of us all brought a raincoat. We carefully walked up the stairs flowing with rushing water like a waterfall. It was like going up into another world. At the top was a forest made up of tall, thin trees. A forest not dissimilar to places in Finland or Scandinavia, as Anna Liisa pointed out to us. The place had an otherworldly feel, not your typical Balinese landscape, quite the contrary a misty, mysterious place.

We had our offering and were getting ready as the rain continued to pour down on us. Just as we reached the moment to pray, the rain suddenly stopped. There wasn't much to see in the temple itself, except for a collection of discreet sacred stones gathered around the edges. Unlike the colourful Hindu temples in India with statues galore, the temples in Bali are much more minimalist. It seemed more about the community gathering to pray in them than the décor.

Just before we sat down to pray, I felt a little faint and nearly dropped our offering box on the floor, which is an absolute no-no in Bali, as anything on the floor is deemed as being contaminated. The three of us sat in a row in front of a small altar table where we had placed our offering, Yuni was by my side. She started banging my back with her hand, while she was chanting a mantra or saying something in Balinese. Suddenly, as soon as our small ceremony came to an end, it started to rain heavily again. We rushed down the river of stairs back to the car, exhausted and ready to go home. This was Bali, always full of surprises.

Early on, when Bali was not yet my home, I would do my visa runs to Australia and catch up with friends and family there. I was lucky to have met some wonderful Australians in Bali and in Australia too. I found them all very kind and hospitable. My aunty Anne in Sydney allowed me to house-sit for a month, while she was in Europe, and I would dog-sit for friends of hers or through a dog-sitting website. Life in Bali seemed to flow. I continued to do a bit of design work for clients in the UK while training in sound therapy. I started writing a blog and my love of photography took me to take photos.

Living in Bali, I had found a piece of wild heaven. The daily blessings, nature, sunshine, jungle and rice paddies filling the landscape with luminous greenery were so uplifting. Being closer to nature and living in this community had been such a gift. Just living here was healing. I met some great friends, which have been my one constant over the last five years. People come and go, but the land is always here, changing and growing. There were always new places to discover, new temples and places around the island to explore, plus smaller islands off the coast of the mainland. I kept on exploring. Last year I lived in Amed in East Bali in a small resort overlooking the sea. It was magical living with an infinite horizon of the sea and views of the island of Lombok.

After a year there, Ubud called me back again. I am now back in my cosy villa, where I had lived several times before. It's tucked behind some rice paddies and a small piece of the jungle on one side. I used to dog-sit a small poodle called Boo here. I had many years of looking after Boo and got to know her owner Rafti. We had met in a local café, Monsieur Spoon. Rafti was sitting nearby, with her long wave of shiny black hair flowing around her face, her arms layered with stunning silver bangles. I found out she was a jewellery designer. Boo was sitting on her lap, as Rafti always wore black, I didn't realise Boo was even there, until all of a sudden a little black poodle jumped down from her lap and came straight over to say hello to me. Well, I fell in love with Boo instantly. I immediately offered my services as a dog-sitter and told Rafti how much I loved looking after cats and especially dogs. Soon after I started to look after Boo, whenever Rafti went on her regular trips to Europe.

Back in 2018, I moved in and shared with Rafti and Boo. I had the upstairs room and from my window, I can see the glorious Mount Agung, the country's most sacred mountain. At sunrise and in the evening, I'd often sit on the balcony overlooking the jungle and would watch the trees, a mixture of banana leaves and different shaped leaves, swaying in the breeze. My favourite tree was a huge heart-shaped one among the canopy of green. How blessed I felt living here. Feeling close to nature with all the early-morning sounds of the birds, squirrels and other forest creatures. Boo was the happiest, most well-mannered and playful of dogs. I would take her on walks along our street and whenever we met the local Bali dogs I'd whisk her up into my arms protectively. Bali street dogs are friendly, but I didn't want to take any chances. Rafti also had Echo, a gorgeous little tabby cat and rat catcher when required, although she was very noisy and would meow for food all the time. Recently Echo has adopted me as her own and has changed her character into a more home loving affectionate cat.

Along a narrow path to my house, past the rice paddies, as you walk along butterflies and dragonflies always appear out of the rows of bushes and flowers and brush past you as if to greet you. The main entrance has two beautifully carved wooden doors with scenes of Rama and Sita, the god and goddess who are united in love. The place is modern but includes some Balinese-style flourishes in the design. As you enter the walled garden, you are surrounded by all shades of green plants and a blaze of pink and purple flowering vines around a swimming pool, a little oasis of tranquillity I call home. Each day as I relax by the pool, at 5 pm sharp I see the silver dragonfly creating her geometric shapes around the pool and skimming across the water. Sometimes I have to pinch myself that I have found such beauty and peace here, a world away from my life in the UK. I have found my own path and created my own wonderland. As I drive my motorbike, each morning through the streets of my adopted hometown, I feel blessed and remind myself that holding on to my dream of finding a new way of living has happened and I am filled with gratitude.

This is the gift that I was told I would receive, the gift of a whole new life on this magical island.

Afterward

A woman I had met on my travels in India, said to me, "Live your life without judgement, with no expectations and no conclusions." I have been consciously reminding myself of this phrase ever since.

When we go through traumatic events, it's a time for our souls to grow. I believe it's a life lesson that we choose no matter how hard it is, and it came to us, as we are able to deal with it. We live with the unknown and break through the barriers, becoming wiser and more compassionate human beings. Sometimes we must stand alone and other times we reach out for help. That's why I am sharing my story. I have gained knowledge about how to help myself and others on their path of facing difficult and painful experiences.

Our lives are unique, but our experiences are universal, and I hope by sharing mine I can help others receive the support they need and accept it's just another human experience that can connect us to a more authentic version of ourselves. I feel that whatever happens in our lives prepares us for the next step. I can look back now and see how my past has shaped me and prepared me for the future. We can live through these apparent negative experiences and discover new ways to resolve issues around shame, guilt, alienation, abandonment, grief, and loss.

Life is full of adventures and that certainly goes for mine. We never know where it will take us. Sunny and optimistic, I was the least likely of people to end up being sectioned in a psych ward, but it happened due to the unusual circumstances I found myself in. Having my freedom taken from me and being forcibly drugged taught me a lot. I saw so many parallels with what is happening in the world today. It taught me resilience and challenged me on every level. Having a spiritual awakening through my losses made me a perfect candidate in western society to be sectioned. I was not mad but suffering from grief and shock from my sudden loss. The stigma of being locked up, and the shame and embarrassment of the whole episode had a knock-on effect. I discovered that accepting the unknown and trusting myself was the key to making the most of life. It certainly hasn't been easy, but it pushed me to the edge to find happiness within myself and in my life.

Living in Bali for the last five years has helped me enormously as I discovered a new way to live, away from the western world, without the crushing pressures and anxieties, but living in communities that care for each other. I got to explore a different culture, explore more music, sound, and retrained in sound therapy. I met new people who had similar experiences and found the support and space I needed to create another life for myself. I live closer to nature, overlooking rice fields and jungle views full of tropical trees. Living in a home surrounded by nature and shimmering in the sunshine helps a lot, too. I spent some time living by the coast and soft-sandy beaches, infinite horizons, the sky, clouds, and views of nearby islands. This deeper connection I have created with nature has brought me so much joy and happiness. Nature is the key—it teaches us what we need to know and the future of life on this earth. I feel at home here, and I love to drive through the streets of my town, feeling blessed that I was given this opportunity to call Bali home and have Echo, my gorgeous cat, to care for. I found a love for caring for animals. I haven't found the lovely man yet, or the dog–although I did have the pleasure of caring for Rafti's dog Boo over the years.

What I learned from living in this tropical paradise is that home is not defined by the place you grow up and where your family is, but it's the place where your heart takes you and where you feel comfortable being yourself.

Life is a circle, and everything comes back to the self. No matter where you travel you are always with yourself. I finally found the peace and joy I needed to live a simpler, happier life on my own.

I heard this quote by RD Laing recently and it made a lot of sense to me: "We never see another person's experience; all we see is their behaviour.

Author's Note

"A normal reaction to an abnormal situation"

Trauma is a process we will all go through at some point in our lives, either alone, or collectively in the society we live in. This book is my experience of a complex trauma which created a spiritual emergency, that had a domino effect on all aspects of my life, including my personal freedom and health.

Spiritual awakening is often linked to a traumatic or life-changing experience. The trauma I went through, ignited my own instant spiritual awakening; through the sudden painful loss of my adopted children and divorce creating the subsequent events. Some traumas are slower in their evolution, but I believe some of us need a faster transformation. It is my belief we have chosen to experience this on a soul level, to get us on the right pathway. The emotions attached to our traumatic experiences in western society are often pushed down and we are shamed into submission, masking our guilty secrets of suffering and pain.

Life is a series of stories, and this is part of mine. As human beings our stories need to be heard to help others and ourselves. We are validated by our human emotions, and we can become whole. We connect with our higher divine self and become the multi-dimensional beings we truly are. This is hopefully an example of how we can take control and change to live our imperfectly perfect life!

Useful References

The Kubler Ross Curve. Charts the steps of change
The Five Stages of Grief, Elizabeth Kubler-Ross
Death and Dying, Elizabeth Kubler-Ross
The Power of Now, Eckhart Tolle
The Artists Way, Julia Cameroon
Visioning, Lucia Cappriohnne
The Work of Bryon Katie by Bryon Katie
or view online her worksheet: www.thework.com
The Art of Happiness, Dalai Lama
Healing Mantras, Thomas Ashley-Farrand
Inner Engineering, Sadhguru
Gabor Mate, When the Body Says No,
The Cost of Hidden Stress
The Body Keeps the Score: Brain, Mind, and Body in the Healing of Trauma, Bessel Van De Kolk
Kundalini Yoga Experience, Bringing Body, Mind, and Spirit Together Guru Dharam S Khalsa and Darryl O'Keefe
Kundalini Yoga Detox and Destress with Maya Fiennes (DVD)
EMDR Therapy
Dr Sam Watts | www.mind-body-medical.co.uk
Ayuveda Health Home, Nepal | https://ayurveda.com.np

Author Bio

Alice was born in London, United Kingdom. Her parents moved to the south coast of England as a child, but she returned to London and lived all her adult life there. After studying art history and film studies she became a Bass Player in a semi-successful Indie Band, called The Auteurs alongside her then boyfriend. Early on they toured with Brit Pop band Suede, and David Gray, making 4 albums during their career and touring the world. During this time Alice developed her love of photography and later in her 30's moved into magazine publishing, creating photo shoots, and working as a photographic agent. In her 40's she moved out of London, got married and retrained as a graphic designer.

Since 2017 she found a new home in Bali, after travelling various countries and she never left. She has come full circle back to music, retraining in sound healing, playing harmonium, singing mantra, and working with voice and frequencies.

For more information on my work and links to useful information you can visit the following websites:

www.iamalicebook.com
Insta: @iamalicebook
https://travelwithalice.com
Insta: @travelwith_alice
Podcast on Podbean: I am Alice

Acknowledgements

A special thank you to my siblings and all of my family as I couldn't have come through life without your support, kindness and encouragement.

From my life in the UK: Sandra P, Martin & Pat, Marion, Julia Mac, Cleo, Kerrie C, Michelle F, Prudence, Monica, Jenni, Carol, Sarah Mc, Sally, Gabrielle C, Caroline G, Linda Jarrrett & Chris Jarrett, Sarah Joy Williams RIP

To the friends I met along the way: Michelle P, Tjasa, Rafti and Boo, Echo, Yuni, Anna Liisa, Ursula, Peter & Lynn, Didi, Chris P, Ann S, Bobbie F, Alison R, Julia C, & Catherine S, Ciara Mc, & Diane H.

Thank you for advice, inspiration, and guidance: Dr Misra, Dr Sam Watts, Dr Rumee, Dr Rishi RIP, Ann Beazer RIP, Master Ketut Arsana, Mama & Agung and Noviana Kusumawardhani

Thank you to Sarah Bonnar for the Cover Design
www.sarahbonnar.co.uk

An extra special thanks to my editor Britt Collins
www.brittcollins.net

Ho'oponopono Prayer

I am sorry
Please forgive me
I love you
Thank you

I would like to honour my unborn children, who are my little soul stars in the sky.

Much love goes to the two beautiful children, who I couldn't adopt. I wish them peace, joy, and happiness in their lives wherever they are. They weren't meant for me in this lifetime, but we had a soul connection. You both changed my life forever. I thank you and I'm truly sorry for any further suffering you may have endured.

To all the people I met along the way that touched my heart and we didn't even know each other, but you made a difference to me. A heartfelt thank you.

Lokah Samastah Sukhino Bhavantu
May all beings everywhere be happy and free

Peace & Love
Alice x

Printed in Great Britain
by Amazon

24697540R00123